T0306477

The Perennial Philosophy

Series

About Ananda K. Coomaraswamy

"Among those who are responsible not only for the Indian Renaissance but for a new Renaissance in the world, Dr. Ananda Coomaraswamy holds a preeminent position. It is my hope that students who are now led away by the passing fashions of our age will turn to his writings for a proper orientation."
—**Sir Sarvepalli Radhakrishnan**, former President of India (1962-1967), author of *The Hindu View of Life*

"[Ananda Coomaraswamy is] that noble scholar upon whose shoulders we are still standing."
—**Heinrich Zimmer**, author of *The King and the Corpse* and *Philosophies of India*

"[Coomaraswamy] is one of the most learned and creative scholars of the century."
—**Mircea Eliade**, author of *Myth and Reality* and editor-in-chief of *The Encyclopedia of Religion*

"Coomaraswamy's essays [give] us a view of his scholarship and brilliant insight."
—**Joseph Campbell**, author of *The Hero with a Thousand Faces* and *The Masks of God*

"Ananda Coomaraswamy is in many ways to me a model: the model of one who has thoroughly and completely united in himself the spiritual tradition and attitudes of the Orient and of the Christian West."
—**Thomas Merton**, author of *The Seven Storey Mountain* and *New Seeds of Contemplation*

"Over sixty years have passed since the death of Ananda Coomaraswamy; yet his writings remain as pertinent today as when he wrote them and his voice echoes in the ears of present day seekers of truth and lovers of traditional art as it did a generation ago. In contrast to most scholarly works which become outmoded and current philosophical opuses which become stale, Coomaraswamy's works possess a timeliness which flows from their being rooted in the eternal present."
—**Seyyed Hossein Nasr**, author of *The Heart of Islam: Enduring Values for Humanity*

"Ananda Coomaraswamy is best known as one of the twentieth century's most erudite and percipient scholars of the sacred arts and crafts of both East and West. He also had few peers in the exegesis of traditional philosophy and metaphysics."
—**Harry Oldmeadow**, author of *Journeys East: 20th Century Western Encounters with Eastern Religious Traditions*

"Coomaraswamy's essays, learned, elegant, and wise, are one of the great treasures of twentieth-century thought. To read them is to see the world in the clear light of tradition, to understand art and philosophy from the viewpoint of first principles, to be reminded of our sacred calling and of the One who calls us."
—**Philip Zaleski**, editor of *The Best Spiritual Writing* series

"Ananda K. Coomaraswamy is in the very first rank of exceptional men, such as René Guénon and Frithjof Schuon, who in our 'dark age' have permitted us to rediscover the great truths of sacred Tradition, to relearn what a civilization, a society, and a world are that conform to this Tradition.... The masterful work of Ananda K. Coomaraswamy is one of the most suitable to enlighten the minds and hearts of 'men of good will.'"
—**Jean Hani**, author *The Symbolism of the Christian Temple* and *Divine Craftsmanship*

"Coomaraswamy uncovers and puts before us the truths of a primordial tradition, reflected in the world's existing traditions and expressed by them as if in differing dialects. He asks us to join him in the effort to decipher the religiously rich arts and crafts, literatures and folklore of the world's traditions."
—**Roger Lipsey**, author of *Coomaraswamy: His Life and Work*

"Others have written the truth about life and religion and man's work. Others have written good clear English. Others have had the gift of witty exposition. Others have understood the metaphysics of Christianity and others have understood the metaphysics of Hinduism and Buddhism. Others have understood the true significance of erotic drawings and sculptures. Others have seen the relationships of the true and the good and the beautiful. Others have had apparently unlimited learning. Others have loved; others have been kind and generous. But I know of no one else in whom all these gifts and all these powers have been combined.... I believe that no other living writer has written the truth in matters of art and life and religion and piety with such wisdom and understanding."
—**Eric Gill**, sculptor and typeface designer

World Wisdom

The Library of Perennial Philosophy

The Library of Perennial Philosophy is dedicated to the exposition of the timeless Truth underlying the diverse religions. This Truth, often referred to as the *Sophia Perennis*—or Perennial Wisdom—finds its expression in the revealed Scriptures as well as the writings of the great sages and the artistic creations of the traditional worlds.

The Wisdom of Ananda Coomaraswamy appears as one of our selections in the Perennial Philosophy series.

The Perennial Philosophy Series

In the beginning of the twentieth century, a school of thought arose which has focused on the enunciation and explanation of the Perennial Philosophy. Deeply rooted in the sense of the sacred, the writings of its leading exponents establish an indispensable foundation for understanding the timeless Truth and spiritual practices which live in the heart of all religions. Some of these titles are companion volumes to the Treasures of the World's Religions series, which allows a comparison of the writings of the great sages of the past with the perennialist authors of our time.

The Wisdom of Ananda Coomaraswamy

Reflections on Indian Art, Life, and Religion

Edited by

S. Durai Raja Singam

&

Joseph A. Fitzgerald

Introduction by

Whitall N. Perry

World Wisdom

The Wisdom of Ananda Coomaraswamy:
Reflections on Indian Art, Life, and Religion

Library of Congress Cataloging-in-Publication Data

Coomaraswamy, Ananda Kentish, 1877-1947.
The wisdom of Ananda Coomaraswamy : reflections on Indian art, life, and religion / edited by S. Durai Raja Singam & Joseph A. Fitzgerald ; introduction by Whitall N. Perry.
p. cm. -- (The perennial philosophy series)
Based on the work published by Singam in 1979.
Includes bibliographical references and index.
ISBN 978-1-935493-95-2 (pbk. : alk. paper) 1. Art. 2. India--Civilization. I. Raja Singam, S. Durai. II. Fitzgerald, Joseph A., 1977- III. Raja Singam, S. Durai. Wisdom of Ananda Coomaraswamy. 1979. IV. Title.
N7445.2.C68 2011
954--dc22

2011007548

Cover art: Siva Nataraja

Printed on acid-free paper in China

For information address World Wisdom, Inc.
P.O. Box 2682, Bloomington, Indiana 47402-2682
www.worldwisdom.com

CONTENTS

EDITOR'S NOTE

In 1946, S. Durai Raja Singam published, in a limited cyclostyled edition, a collection of quotations selected from the writings, letters, and speeches of the late Ananda K. Coomaraswamy. The book went through three mimeographed editions before 1979, when Singam printed 350 copies of the book, which, along with two other titles, he distributed free of cost. "I have published these books at my own cost," Singam explains, "in memory of my beloved son Dr. Ananda Krishna Coomaraswamy, who was named after Dr. Ananda Kentish Coomaraswamy, and blessed by him on his birth." In 2001, after Singam's death, the book was reprinted in India by Indica Books. It has not, until now, been published outside India.

The present edition preserves the core of Singam's work, while making some alterations to the presentation and content. Certain passages have been deleted and others have been added, taken primarily from Coomaraswamy's mature writings on metaphysics and symbolism. New illustrations have also been added. The numbers in brackets after each selection refer to the source publication, a key to which is provided at the end of the volume. A bracketed asterisk at the end of a quotation indicates that that the source is not known.

JOSEPH A. FITZGERALD

Ananda K. Coomaraswamy in 1937

PREFACE[1]

The mind that Coomaraswamy turned upon life was insatiate, roving like a bee to suck the essence of every blossom of thought or fancy, but unerringly making a bee-line to bear back honey to his wisdom's hive.

Joseph T. Shipley

Ananda Kentish Coomaraswamy was born on August 22, 1877, the only child of Ceylon Tamil lawyer, Sir Mutu Coomaraswamy, and Englishwoman Elizabeth Clay Beeby. Ananda and Elizabeth went to England in 1878, but in 1879, before he was able to join his wife and son in England, Sir Mutu—the first Hindu allowed to the bar in England and the first Asian knighted by the English throne—died in Ceylon. Although Ananda was educated in England, he never forgot his Asian heritage.

Ananda Coomaraswamy's first interest was science. He spent some six years at Wycliffe College in Gloucestershire and then went to the University of London for a B.Sc. in geology and botany with first class honors. He took this knowledge back to Ceylon to head the first mineralogical survey of that area as the Director of Mineralogical Research for Ceylon from 1903-1906. He discovered the mineral thorianite in Ceylon, and he was awarded a D.Sc. degree for his geological studies during this time.

Having returned to the culture of his heritage, Coomaraswamy became interested in a program of national education in India. He was appalled at what British education was doing to the Asian culture in India. A series of essays about these issues began a long and fruitful career of scholarly and forceful writing.

As part of the culture Coomaraswamy sought to restore, the arts and crafts of India became a focus for him. He toured India extensively in 1910 and collected one of the finest collections of art and crafts ever exhibited. At the United Provinces Exhibition in Allahabad in 1911, Coomaraswamy presented this collection as he was put in charge of the Art Section. In 1917,

[1] Editor's Note: The following combines and edits two introductory pieces written by S. Durai Raja Singam.

during World War I, Coomaraswamy took his collection to the Museum of Fine Arts, Boston, where he accepted the position of Keeper of Indian Art in the Department of Asiatic, Islamic, and Near Eastern Arts. He remained there until his death, September 9, 1947.

Coomaraswamy wrote many fine critiques of art, but more and more he looked to art as a key to understanding metaphysics. He was responsible for some of the finest interpretations of Hinduism, Buddhism, and the religious literature of his culture, as well as interpretations of the spiritual values demonstrated in the artwork of India which have ever been written.

Had he not died in 1947, Coomaraswamy would have retired from the museum and gone to live in the Himalayas in 1948. Already he had begun to turn away from museum activities toward a more spiritual existence. He left undone many works he had planned, and yet from the early scientific studies, to the political articles and books, to the translations of spiritual works and songs, to the critiques of art, and finally to the many works in metaphysical aspects of art and life, Coomaraswamy completed literally hundreds of works, each in his crisp and precise style of scholarly demonstration of truth from source documentation.

These selections in thematic arrangement had its beginnings in 1946 and had the blessings of Ananda Coomaraswamy. A typed copy of more than two-thirds of these selections were sent to him for his approval which he readily and kindly gave.[2] When this anthology of selections first appeared in 1946 (in a limited cyclostyled edition), it attracted wide interest among general readers as well as students of art and philosophy. These selections of nearly a thousand cover in brief a wide range of subjects and bear witness to Coomaraswamy's wisdom and insight. As one progresses in their study one is often left with a thirst for a fuller and detailed account and one day a complete edition of Coomaraswamy's works must be done.

[2] In fact Coomaraswamy wrote to me to omit one selection, for his views on that topic had changed. "I would not say that now," he wrote. "I have used the tools of the present age, that is my scientific training, which I took seriously, to be used without a bias. My life, my work, and my understanding follow a sequence and are predominantly logical." It is always best to be cautious when quoting these utterances emphasizing their contextual origins. One should not judge a saying on a fixed mold of immutability.

I am grateful to Mr. Whitall N. Perry for his introduction. Coomaraswamy brought me to friends I knew not previously, friends in different lands whom I have never met. Perry's *A Treasury of Traditional Wisdom*[3] is a great book. In 1946, he came under the close personal influence of Coomaraswamy, whose hope for a Summa of the *Philosophia Perennis* gave the original impetus for this book that fulfilled Coomaraswamy's wish within a quarter of a century of his uttering it.

Ananda Coomaraswamy had an inexhaustibly fertile mind and though he himself declared that life is not long enough for the achievement of many different things, it is the great versatility in his work that strikes us first as we read the varied titles of his vast output. His is the kind of mind that brings together separate areas of knowledge into an almost visionary illumination of the pattern of reality, the "Gods," which underlies the kaleidoscope of life and activity and gives significance to all one's piecemeal explorations in the various "fields of knowledge." "I am wholly convinced," he declares in his essay, "The Religious Basis of the Forms of Indian Society," "that there is one truth that shines through . . . all in many shapes, a truth greater in glory by far than can be circumscribed by any creed or circumscribed by the walls of any church or temple." These selections have been an attempt to give a glimpse into this great truth which Ananda Coomaraswamy perceived, in the hope of luring the reader to a recognition of the great sage and the existence of his work.

S. Durai Raja Singam

[3] Published by Quinta Essentia, Cambridge, 1971, and Indica Books, Varanasi, 1998 (this last edition for sale only in South Asia). [Editor's Note: It was later retitled *The Spiritual Ascent: A Compendium of the World's Wisdom* (Louisville, KY: Fons Vitae, 2008).]

Surya chariot, Konarak Sun temple, Orissa

INTRODUCTION

One often speaks of the "Greek miracle"; but who ever hears of the miracle of Hinduism, this extraordinary amalgam of Proto-Australoid, Mongolian, Negrito, and notably Dravidian and Aryan cultures anciently established on the Indian sub-continent, that flowered at some cyclical moment prior to recorded history into the brilliant homogeneous spiritual-socio-ethnic system we still know today, and whose essence is the *Sanatana Dharma* or perpetual *Veda*? Traveling in India at the beginning of the Christian era, Apollonius of Tyana found that "Pythagoras was anticipated by the Indians." Yet Pythagoras himself antedated the Hellenistic period in question, which so far from being "miraculous" was more truly a waning segment of the Aryan tradition, and which in unison with Roman culture was to father that humanism whose post-Christian and "posthumous vengeance"—in the words of Frithjof Schuon—erupted as the European Renaissance with its civilizationist aberrations culminating in the materialistic, relativistic, and tamasic anomalies of the twentieth century. This, then, is the background against which Ananda K. Coomaraswamy has so tellingly raised his voice and witness.

Hindu sages proclaim that the eternal *Veda* will alone endure, being the universal substratum of all religious forms: and in this sense—as well as historically and geographically—Hinduism is providentially situated as a sort of "axis" among world religions; and Coomaraswamy in his turn, given his profound intellectual substance and vision, has been admirably destined through his East-West origins to remanifest this worldwide nature of the *Sanatana Dharma*. He brings the Indian heritage to the West, while pointing the West back to her own traditional birthright—Christian and pre-Christian; and the universality of this outlook enables him to draw on "all orthodox sources whatever" of the *Philosophia Perennis* to compose a unified world picture of the "normal" order of things, which is the prerogative of no one single people or religion anywhere.

These present extracts of Coomaraswamy's writings, chosen from the heart and judiciously arranged by Sri S. Durai Raja Singam, serve beyond the immediate merit of their didactic message a twofold purpose: they reveal intimate facets of the more personal side of Coomaraswamy; we behold the "structure" of his own thoughts and attitudes and aspirations; we see the man behind the Doctor. And secondly, one cannot fail to hear an appeal of urgent concern—a crucial call to India to remain Indian.

For in the quarter of a century since his death,[1] the ravages he foresaw have devastatingly increased on a global scale; and although one may demur before Professor A.K. Saran's pronouncement that "today there is no *living* Hindu society in India," nevertheless how many contemporary Hindus could pass muster by the criterion of K.V. Rangaswami Aiyangar: "He who rejects *Dharmasastra*, especially where its dicta rest on Vedic sanction, is not therefore a Hindu"? And Coomaraswamy would certainly be the first to endorse the words of Sri Chandrasekhara Bharati Swamigal, the late Sankaracharya of Sringeri: "It is well known that people everywhere are now suffering. It can be confidently asserted that this suffering dates from their giving up the courses of conduct observed by their ancestors. When the practice of *Dharma* began to decline, suffering began."

It must be stressed that Coomaraswamy's love for India transcended any political or nationalistic bias, and was based on a veneration for the sacred and the noble in a form that has a genius for translating first principles into scriptures and art patterns haunting in their beauty. I knew the Doctor at the time when India was just gaining independence. He could attend rallies with no taint of "patriotism," as he told me, since any nationalistic fervor had long since ceded to the *contemptus mundi* of his spiritual detachment—he who had truly learned to find himself, "'in place' anywhere, and 'at home' everywhere—in the profoundest sense, a citizen of the world."

It is not hard to see from the allusion to beauty just above, how the genius in the tradition fired the genius in the sage with an impassioned love for art forms, which extended to the principles of art in all traditions. It took Coomaraswamy's acid pen to quash modern society's narcissistic infatuation with "art for art's sake" through the sobering *mise au point* that "the artist is not a special kind of man, but every man a special kind of artist." Images (icons), he tells us, are not made to be seen (exhibited) but *realized*; thus originally they were not "works of art" but "means (*sadhana*) of edification." Hence "an image will not represent a moment of time, but a condition of being" (and if we evaluate much contemporary "art" by this criterion, we see that this "condition of being" more often than not is a pathological concatenation of psychic fissures unmasking a wasteland of the soul). Only that is truly beautiful—and real—which accords with revealed and established canons and not with individual fancies!

[1] Editor's Note: Now more than half a century ago.

This, then, is the Coomaraswamy that Sri Singam presents to us, a portrait of the man shaped in the ardor of his own ideals, his intransigence regarding canons and principles of art, his deep love of and dedication to that true India which modernized Indians would so easily betray in their blind fascination with the West's shabby materialism, and his equally profound understanding of and respect for Platonism and mediaeval Christian culture—as part of the whole Universal perspective to which his heart really belonged. But the stress on India makes this collection of extracts particularly valuable for Indians—Hindus first of all, and Muslims by extension. And since India plays a chosen role among world faiths, we all—Buddhists, Christians, Sikhs, Jainas, Taoists and the rest—,will be enabled to find that particular aspect of Coomaraswamy's message which best accords with our own predestined path.

WHITALL N. PERRY

Ananda K. Coomaraswamy in the 1930s

Ananda K. Coomaraswamy in the 1940s

SEVENTIETH BIRTHDAY ADDRESS[1]

I am more than honored—somewhat, indeed, overcome—by your kindness in being here tonight, by the messages that have been read, and by the Presentation of Mr. Bharatha Iyer's *festschrift*.[2] I should like to recall the names of four who might have been present had they been living: Dr. Denman W. Ross, Dr. John Lodge, Dr. Lucien Scherman, and Professor James Woods, to all of whom I am indebted. The formation of the Indian collection in the Museum of Fine Arts was almost wholly due to the initiative of Dr. Denman Ross; Dr. Lodge, who wrote little, will be remembered for his work in Boston and Washington, and also perhaps for his aphorism: "From the Stone Age until now, *quelle dégringolade*.[3]" I still hope to complete a work on reincarnation with which Dr. Scherman charged me not long before his death; and Professor Woods was one of those teachers who can never be replaced.

More than half of my active life has been spent in Boston. I want to express my gratitude in the first place to the Directors and Trustees of the Museum of Fine Arts, who have always left me entirely free to carry on research not only in the field of Indian art but at the same time in the wider field of the whole traditional theory of art and of the relation of man to his work, and in the fields of comparative religion and metaphysics to which the problems of iconography are a natural introduction. I am grateful also to the American Oriental Society whose editors, however much they differed from me "by temperament and training" as Professor Norman Brown once said, have always felt that I had "a right to be heard," and have allowed me to be heard. And all this despite the fact that such studies as I have made necessarily led me back to an enunciation of relatively unpopular sociological doctrines. For, as a student of human manufactures, aware that all making

[1] Editor's Note: Dr. Ananda Coomaraswamy read the following speech, the last of his life, on the occasion of his 70th birthday at Boston on August 22, 1947, a few days before his death on September 9th 1947. The full text of this speech was sent by Ananda Coomaraswamy to me, a few days before his death.

[2] Editor's Note: The *festschrift* was later published as *Art and Thought: A Volume in Honour of the Late Dr. Ananda K. Coomaraswamy* (London: Luzac and Co., 1947).

[3] Editor's Note: "What a downfall."

is *per artem,*[4] I could not but see that, as Ruskin said, "Industry without art is brutality," and that men can never be really happy unless they bear an individual responsibility not only for what they do but for the kind and the quality of whatever they make. I could not fail to see that such happiness is forever denied to the majority under the conditions of making that are imposed upon them by what is euphemistically called "free enterprise," that is to say, under the condition of production for profit rather than for use; and no less denied in those totalitarian forms of society in which the folk is just as much as in a capitalistic regime reduced to the level of the proletariat. Looking at the works of art that are considered worthy of preservation in our museums, and that were once the common objects of the market place, I could not but realize that a society can only be considered truly civilized when it is possible for every man to earn his living by the very work he would rather be doing than anything else in the world—a condition that has only been attained in social orders integrated on the basis of vocation, *svadharma*.

At the same time I should like to emphasize that I have never built up a philosophy of my own or wished to establish a new school of thought. Perhaps the greatest thing I have learned is never to think for myself: I fully agree with André Gide that "toutes choses sont dites déjà,"[5] and what I have sought is to understand what has been said, while taking no account of the "inferior philosophers." Holding with Heraclitus that the Word is common to all, and that Wisdom is to know the Will whereby all things are steered, I am convinced with Jeremias that the human cultures in all their apparent diversity are but the dialects of one and the same language of the spirit,[6] that there is a "common universe of discourse" transcending the differences of tongues.

This is my seventieth birthday, and my opportunity to say: Farewell. For this is our plan, mine and my wife's, to retire and return to India next year; thinking of this as an *astam gamana,* "going home." There we expect to rejoin our son Rama, who, after traveling with Marco Pallis in Sikkim and speaking Tibetan there, is now at the Gurukula Kangri learning Sanskrit and Hindi with the very man, Pandit Vagishvarji, with whom my wife was

[4] Editor's Note: "By skill" or "by craft."

[5] Editor's Note: "Everything has already been said."

[6] Editor's Note: "Human culture is a unitary whole, and its separate cultures are the dialects of one and the same language of the spirit" (Alfred Jeremias, *Handbuch der Altorientalischen Geisteskultur* [Berlin, 1929], chap XVII, p. 508).

studying there twelve years ago. We mean to remain in India, now a free country, for the rest of our lives.

I have not remained untouched by the religious philosophies I have studied and to which I was led by way of the history of art, *Intellige ut credas*![7] In my case, at least, understanding has involved belief; and for me the time has come to exchange the active for a more contemplative way of life in which it would be my hope to experience more immediately, more fully at least a part of the truth of which my understanding has been so far predominantly logical. And so, though I may be here for another year, I ask you also to say "Good bye"—equally in the etymological sense of the word and in that of the Sanskrit *svaga*, a salutation that expresses the wish "May you come into your own," that is, may I know and become what I am, no longer this man So-and-so, but the Self that is also the Being of all beings, my Self and your Self.

Ananda K. Coomaraswamy in the 1940s

[7] Editor's Note: "Understand in order to believe."

1. SOCIETY

Lion Capital of Asoka, adopted as the National Emblem of India, Sarnath, Uttar Pradesh, 3rd century

INDIA

Before we can have India, we must become Indians. . . . I firmly believe the only service possible to render to the cause of Indian freedom is service to Indian ideas. (75)

No one can say that any such idea as that of a Federated States of India is altogether foreign to the Indian mind. But more than all this, there is evidence enough that the founders of Indian culture and civilization and religion (whether you call them *rishis* or men) had this unity in view; and the manner in which this idea pervades the whole of Indian culture is the explanation of the possibility of its rapid realization now. Is it for nothing that India's sacred shrines are many and far apart; that one who would visit more than one or two of these must pass over hundreds of miles of Indian soil? Benares is the sacred city of Buddhist, and Hindu alike; Samanala in Ceylon is a holy place for Buddhist, Hindu, and Muhammadan. Is there no meaning in the sacred reverence for the Himalayas which every Indian feels? Is the *geis* [taboo] altogether meaningless which forbids the orthodox Hindu to leave the Motherland and cross the seas? Is the passionate adoration of the Indian people for the Ganges thrown away? How much is involved in such phrases as "The Seven Great Rivers" (of India)! The Hindu in the north repeats the *mantram*:

> *Om gange ca yamune caiva godavari sarasvati*
> *narmade sindhu kaveri jalesmin samnidhim kuru*[1]

when performing ceremonial ablutions; the Buddhist in Ceylon uses the same prayer on a similar occasion. Or take the epics, the foundation of Indian education and culture; or a poem like the *Megha Duta*, the best known and most read work of Kalidasa. Are not these expressive of love for and knowledge of the Motherland? The "holy land" of the Indian is not a far-off Palestine but the Indian land itself. (5)

You see, this loss of beauty in our lives is a proof that we do not love India; for India, above all nations, was beautiful not long ago. It is the weakness of our national movement that we do not love India; we love suburban

[1] "Hail, O ye Ganges, Jamna, Godavari, Sarasvati, Narmada, Sindhu and Kaveri, come and approach these waters."

England, we love the comfortable bourgeois prosperity that is to be some day established when we have learned enough science and forgotten enough art to successfully compete with Europe in a commercial war conducted on its present lines. It is not thus that nations are made. (76)

I am often reminded of the Cairene girl's lute, in the tale of Miriam and Ali Nur al-Din. It was kept in "green satin bag with slings of gold." She took the bag "and opening it, shook it, where upon there fell thereout two-and-thirty pieces of wood, which she fitted one into other, male into female and female into male, till they became a polished lute of Indian workmanship. Then she uncovered her wrists and laying the lute in her lap, bent over it with the bending of mother over babe, and swept the strings with her fingertips; whereupon it moaned and resounded and after its olden home yearned; and it remembered the waters that gave it drink and the earth whence it sprang and wherein it grew and it minded the carpenters who cut it and the polishers who polished it and the merchants who made it their merchandise and the ships that shipped it; and it cried and called aloud and moaned and groaned; and it was as if she asked it of all these things and it answered her with the tongue of the case." Just such an instrument is India, composed of many parts seemingly irreconcilable, but in reality each one cunningly designed towards a common end; so, too, when these parts are set together and attuned, will India tell of the earth from which she sprang, the waters that gave her drink, and the Shapers that have shaped her being; nor will she be then the idle singer of an empty day, but the giver of hope to all, when hope will most avail, and most be needed. (5)

The whole of Indian culture is so pervaded with this idea of India as THE LAND, that it has never been necessary to insist upon it overmuch, for no one could have supposed it otherwise. (55)

Indian culture is valid not so much because it is Indian as because it is culture. At the same time its special forms are adapted to a specifically Indian nature and inheritance, and they are appropriate to us in the same way that a national dress is appropriate to those who have a right to wear it. We cut a sorry figure in our foreign or hybrid clothes; and only invite the ridicule of foreign musicians for imitating their vulgarisms, such as the harmonium. (35)

We believe in India for the Indians but if we do so, it is not merely because we want our own India for ourselves, but because we believe that every nation has its own part to play in the long tale of human progress, and that nations which are not free to develop their own individuality and own character are also unable to make the contribution to the sum of human culture which the world has a right to expect of them. We are not merely striving for a right, but accepting a duty that is binding on us, that of self-realization to the utmost for the sake of others. (5)

Have you ever thought that India politically and economically free, but subdued by Europe in her inmost soul, is scarcely an ideal to be dreamt of or to live or die for. (4)

The inspiration of our nationalism must be not hatred or self-seeking: but love, first of India, and secondly of England and of the world. The highest ideal of nationality is service: and it is because this service is impossible for us so long as we are politically and spiritually dominated by any Western civilization, that we are bound to achieve our freedom. It is in this spirit that we must say to Englishmen, that we will achieve this freedom, if they will, with their consent and with their help: but if they will not, then without their consent and in spite of their resistance. (5)

This brings us to the last part of this address, viz., the consideration of practical steps that may be taken to bring us into closer touch with India. There is, first, the study of Indian history and literature essential, in any case, to the right appreciation of our own. Equal in importance to this education of the historical sense in us, is the need for the education of the geographical sense. In former times this was to some extent accomplished by means of religious pilgrimages. These are less often undertaken now and the easier means of conveyance available lessen the educational value also. Nevertheless, traveling in India is the very best method of putting oneself in touch with modern Indians. In the course of a tour in India recently, I have everywhere found a welcome for one from distant parts and have been much struck by the great strengthening of the feeling of brotherhood and unity in India and strengthening of the Indian idea generally, which may result from more extended acquaintances amongst Indians from distant parts. Misapprehensions are removed and friendships made. On this account and on account of the educational value of such travel, no Indian or Ceylonese should deem his Indian education complete, if he has not, very much in the pilgrim spirit, visited some of the historic sites of India, and made the acquaintances of other Indian peoples. Such travel would be of far more value for instance, than a hasty visit to Europe. (1)

As regards India, it has been said that "East is East and West is West, and never the twain shall meet." This is a counsel of despair, that can only have been born of the most profound disillusion and deepest conviction of impotence. I say on the contrary that human nature is an unchanging and everlasting principle; and that whoever possesses such a nature—and not merely the outward form and the habits of the human animal—is endowed with the power of understanding all that belongs to that nature, without respect of time or place. (8)

Each race contributes something essential to the world's civilization in the course of its own self-expression and self-realization. The character built up in solving its own problems, in the experience of its own misfortunes is itself a gift which each offers to the world. The essential contribution of India, then, is simply her Indianness; her great humiliation would be to substitute or to have substituted for this own character (*svabhava*) a cosmopolitan veneer for then indeed she must come before the world empty-handed.

A street scene of India in the early 1900s

If now we ask what is most distinctive in this essential contribution, we must first make it clear that there cannot be anything absolutely unique in the experience of any race. Its peculiarities will be chiefly a matter of selection and emphasis, certainly not a difference in specific humanity. If we regard the world as a family of nations then we shall best understand the position of India which has passed through many experiences and solved many problems which younger races have hardly yet recognized. The heart and essence of the Indian experience is to be found in a constant intuition of the unity of all life, and the instinctive and ineradicable conviction that the recognition of this unity is the highest good and the uttermost freedom. All that India can offer to the world proceeds from her philosophy. This philosophy is not indeed, unknown to others—it is equally the gospel of Jesus and of Blake, Lao Tzu and Rumi—but nowhere else has it been made the essential basis of sociology and education. (3)

Every race must solve its own problems and those of its own day. I do not suggest that the ancient Indian solutions of the special Indian problems, though its lessons may be many and valuable, can be directly applied to modern conditions. What I do suggest is that the Hindus grasped more firmly than others the fundamental meaning and purpose of life and more deliberately than others organized society with a view to the attainment of the fruit of life; and this organization was designed not for the advantage of a single class, but, to use a modern formula, to take from each according to his capacity and to give to each according to his needs. How far the *rishi*s succeeded in this aim may be a matter of opinion. We must not judge of Indian society, especially Indian society in its present moment of decay, as if it actually realized the Brahmanical social idea; yet even with all its imperfections Hindu society as it survives will appear to many to be superior to any form of social organization attained on a large scale anywhere else, and infinitely superior to the social order which we know as modern civilization.

Gaths at the Ganges

CEYLON

The more I know of Ceylon, the more inseparable from India does it appear, and indeed I regret sometimes that Ceylon and India are not at present under one administration. Ceylon is in the truest sense a part of India. (*)

Of the unity of the Indian peoples, Ceylon is economically, mentally, and spiritually, a part; and with the culture and life of India, must Ceylon's own survive. (7)

India without Ceylon is incomplete.... Ceylon is a more perfect window through which to gaze on India's past than can be found in India itself. Not only are its art and literature and religion free from Muhammadan influence, but they are merely influenced and not completely dominated by later Hindu conceptions, and actually preserve and reflect something of Hindu and Buddhist culture as it existed in that period of mental activity when Asoka just grasped the idea of Indian unity and of fraternity amongst its borders. For very many centuries the relations between South India and Ceylon resembled those between England and France in the early middle ages: alternate warfare and close alliance. The nobler of the two great Indian epics [the *Ramayana*] unites India with Ceylon in the mind of every Indian, and Sita is known from the remotest north of India to the extreme south and there in Ceylon her name is given to many places where she is thought to have rested in her exile. In later times the histories of Northern India and Ceylon were linked by Vijaya's emigration and then by Asoka's mission and later still Padmavati became a Rajput bride and perished by fire like many another Rajput lady when death or dishonor was the only choice; and to this day her name is on the lips of the peoples of Northern India as the very flower and crown of all beauty, even as Deirdre's is in Ireland still. (1)

There is scarcely any part of Sinhalese life, or religion or art, which is quite comprehensible without reference to India; the Sinhalese themselves are Indians, the greatness of their civilization dates from the wave of Indian influences that reached Ceylon through Asoka's missionaries; the air and soil in which the nation has grown and borne good fruit are Indian. (7)

The chief landmarks of the history of Ceylon are the conversion to Buddhism by Asoka's missionaries, the capital at Anuradhapura up to the 8th century; at Polonaruva from the 8th to the 13th century; at Kandy from the

Anuradhapura

Carved Buddhas, Gal Vihara, Polonnaruva, Ceylon

Seated Buddha in Polonnaruva, Vatadage, Ceylon, 12th century

16th century; and the British occupation in 1815. It should be noted that the distinctively Sinhalese (Buddhist) art is the Kandyan art of the interior; the art of Jaffna belongs to that of Southern India while that of the low country during the last three centuries has been one-third European. (6)

Early Buddhism was carried to Ceylon in the time of Asoka (3rd century B.C.) and has remained to this day the religion of the Sinhalese. During the first six centuries A.D. it was taken, in the Brahmanized *Mahayana* form, to China where a great Buddhist art developed on Indian lines; in the 8th century it went with Indian colonists to Java, where are to be seen some of the finest works of Buddhist art in existence. Somewhat later, Buddhist and Hindu art and thought were equally firmly established in Burma, Siam, and Cambodia. (6)

The Ceylonese are painfully given to the imitation of European manners and customs, and those of eating meat and the use of intoxicating drinks have spread far and wide among them. Beside those Buddhists who, while remaining Buddhists, have taken to a meat diet, we have also to consider the Christians. Very few missionaries are themselves vegetarians, or encourage vegetarianism amongst their flock and their converts, and but few native Christians remain vegetarians.… It is no wonder that many Hindus believe that in order to become a true Christian it is necessary to drink intoxicants and eat flesh food. (13)

DRAVIDIANS & ARYANS

The Dravidians are peculiar to India, once universal in India. They are the bearers of a cultural continuity extending from the Stone Age to the present day. Before the second millennium B.C. they formed the bulk of a population thinly scattered throughout India. (*)

The Dravidians developed an early city culture, more ancient than Aryan, perhaps once matriarchal in character. (*)

In India it becomes more than ever clear that thought and culture are due in equal measure both to Aryan and indigenous genius. (68)

The Shore Temple at Mahabalipuram, Tamil Nadu

TRADITION & PROGRESS

The problem of the "spiritual East" versus the "material West" is very easily mistaken; I have repeatedly emphasized that it is only accidentally a geographical or racial problem. The real clash is of traditional with anti-traditional concepts and cultures; and that is unquestionably a clash of spiritual or ideological with material or sensate points of views. Shall we or shall we not delimit sacred and profane departments of life? I, at any rate, will not. I think if you consider Pallis' *Peaks and Lamas* you will see what I mean. I think it undeniable that the *modern* world (which happens to be still a Western world, however fast the East is being Westernized) is one of "impoverished reality" one *entleert* (empty) of meaning, or values. Our contemporary trust in *Progress* is a veritable *fideism* as naive as is to be found in any past historical context. (63)

"East and West" imports a cultural rather than a geographical antithesis: an opposition of the traditional or ordinary way of life that survives in the East to the modern and irregular way of life that now prevails in the West. It is because such an opposition as this could not have been felt before the Renaissance that we say that the problem is one that presents itself only accidentally in terms of geography; it is one of times much more than of places. (14)

The oriental culture and way of life are traditional, the modern antitraditional; the one values stability, the other change or "progress"; one demands from art an adequate expression of truth, the other self-expression; for the one, art is a necessity without which nothing can be well or truly made or adapted to good use; while for the other, art is a luxury to be enjoyed apart from activity and without bearing on conduct. The oriental dance, for example, is an intellectual discipline and physical display or, like other modern arts, the self-expression of the artist's private emotional storms. The oriental artist, even at a court, is really maintained by the unanimous patronage of a unanimous society; the modern artist depends on the precarious support of a clique that is only a tiny fraction of the whole community. As art dealt with the themes which are and have been familiar to everyone, literate or illiterate, and whether rich or poor, for millennia, there had been no necessity to include in cultural curricula courses on "the appreciation of art." When every professional had his disciples or apprentices, there was little need for "school of art" in our sense, but only for masters and pupils. In the East, the necessity for museums was not felt until the traditional arts had been almost destroyed by the contagion of "modern civilization"; just as when folksongs could be heard everywhere, no one "collected" them. (36)

To have set about to "conquer" nature, to have thought of discontent as "divine," to have honored the discoverers of "new wants," to have sacrificed spontaneity to the concept of inevitable "progress"—these positions of the Social Gospel are none of those that the East had ever thought as making for happiness. (57)

The Sinhalese people are not, in my opinion, happier or better than they were in the eighteenth century. Talk of progress, and the reality, are not the same. Civilization is supposed to advance by the creation of new desires, to gratify which the individual must endeavor to improve his position. But in reality it is not quantity, but quality of wants that may be taken as evidence of progress in the Art of Living. No one acquainted with modern Sinhalese taste will pretend that it gives evidence of any improvement in the quality of wants. Indeed, it is sufficiently obvious that quantity, variety, and novelty are not really compatible with quality. (7)

The world's museums are filled with the traditional arts of innumerable peoples whose culture has been destroyed by the sinister power of our industrial civilization: peoples who have been forced to abandon their own highly developed and significant designs in order to preserve their lives by working as hired laborers at the production of raw materials. (24)

Cain, who killed his brother, Abel, the herdsman, and built himself a city, prefigures modern civilization, one that has been described from within as a "murderous machine, with no conscience and no ideals" (G. La Piana), "neither human nor normal nor Christian" (Eric Gill), and in fact "an anomaly, not to say a monstrosity" (René Guénon). It has been said: "The values of life are slowly ebbing. There remains the show of civilization, without any of its realities" (A. N. Whitehead). Criticisms such as these could be cited without end. Modern civilization, by its divorce from any principle, can be likened to a headless corpse of which the last motions are convulsive and insignificant. It is not, however, of suicide, but of murder that we propose to speak. (25)

I am staying in a house in Main Street, a new house with Mangalore tiles. Well, gentlemen, I am often tempted to use an umbrella in the house, so great is the heat that penetrates these tiles. But I have been into some of our old Tamil houses dating from about 100 years ago: immediately on leaving the high road and entering the door, a feeling of coolness is experienced. Besides that, the houses were well and handsomely built with solid timbers, simply carved, and they are fit to stand a hundred years again, but the new house is already showing signs of wear and tear. The difference in coolness is, of course, easily explained; with only one layer of tiles, the sun's heat is transmitted to the air of the room beneath; with four or five of the old tiles, or with a palmyrah thatch, there are layers of air—a non-conductor—which prevent the transmission of heat to the room beneath. Gentlemen, here is a case in which we have not done well in following the dictates of a mere fashion and in exchanging old for new. (1)

The vitality of tradition persists only so long as it is fed by intensity of imagination. (3)

The world may be likened to a vast, as yet unordered garden, having diverse soils and aspects, some watered, some arid, some plain, some mountain; the different parts of which should properly be tended by different gardeners, having experience of diverse qualities of soil and aspect; but certain ones have seized upon the plots of others, and attempted to replace the plants natural to those plots, with others more acceptable or profitable to themselves. We have not to consider only the displaced gardeners, who naturally do not admire and are not grateful for the changes introduced into their plots; but to ask whether these proceedings are beneficial to the owner of the garden for whom the gardeners work. Who is this owner but the Folk of the World of the future, which is ever becoming the present? Shall they be glad or sorry if uniformity has replaced diversity, if but one type of vegetation is to be found within their garden, flourishing perhaps in one part, but sickly in another; what of the flowers that might have flourished in that other part had they not been swept away? (5)

EDUCATION

One of the most remarkable features of British rule in India has been the fact that the greatest injuries done to the people of India have taken the outward form of blessings. Of this, Education is a striking example; for no more crushing blows have ever been struck at the roots of Indian evolution than those which have been struck, often with other, and the best intentions, in the name of Education. It is sometimes said by friends of India that the National movement is the natural result of English education, and one of which England should in truth be proud, as showing that, under "civilization" and the Pax Britannica, Indians are becoming, at last, capable of self-government. The facts are otherwise. If Indians are still capable of self-government, it is in spite of all the anti-national tendencies of a system of education that has ignored or despised almost every ideal informing the national culture. (5)

A single generation of English education suffices to break the threads of tradition and to create a nondescript and superficial being deprived of all roots—a sort of intellectual pariah who does not belong to the East or the West, the past or the future. (3)

It will be for us to develop the Indian intelligence through the medium of Indian culture, and building thereupon, to make it possible for India to resume her place amongst the nations, not merely as a competitor in material production, but as a teacher of all that belongs to a true civilization, a leader of the future, as of the past. Herein the ordinary English educator can help but little, and can hinder much. (5)

It is a marvel to me how a self-respecting people can endure for a day, not the system of government—but the system of education from which we suffer. (4)

None can be true educators of the Indian people who cannot inherit their traditions, or cannot easily work in a spirit of perfect reverence for those traditions. Others can be, not educators, but merely teachers of particular subjects. As such there is still room in India for English teachers; but they should be, not in power, but subordinate; they should be engaged by, paid by, and responsible to Indian managers, as, in Japan, English teachers are responsible to Japanese authorities. (5)

By their fruits ye shall know them. The most crushing indictment of this Education is the fact that it destroys, in the great majority of those upon whom it is inflicted, all capacity for the appreciation of Indian culture. Speak to the ordinary graduate of an Indian University, or a student from Ceylon, of the ideals of the *Mahabharata*—he will hasten to display his knowledge of Shakespeare—; talk to him of religious philosophy—you find that he is an atheist of the crude type common in Europe a generation ago, and that not only has he no religion but he is as lacking in philosophy as the average Englishman—; talk to him of Indian music—he will produce a gramophone or a harmonium, and inflict upon you one or both—; talk to him of Indian dress or jewelry—he will tell you that they are uncivilized and barbaric—; talk to him of Indian art—it is news to him that such a thing exists—; ask him to translate for you a letter written in his own mother tongue—he does not know it.[1] He is indeed a stranger in his own land. (5)

Yes, English educators of India, you do well to scorn the Babu graduate; he is your own special production, made in your own image; he might be one of your very selves. Do you not recognize the likeness? Probably you do not; for you are still hidebound in that impervious skin of self-satisfaction that enabled your most pompous and self-important philistine, Lord Macaulay, to believe that a single shelf of a good European library was worth all the literature of India, Arabia, and Persia. Beware lest in a hundred years the judgment be reversed, in the sense that Oriental culture will occupy a place even in European estimation, ranking at lest equally with Classic. Meanwhile you have done well nigh all that could be done to eradicate it in the land of its birth. (5)

Firstly, the almost universal philosophical attitude, contrasting strongly with that of the ordinary Englishman, who hates philosophy. For every science school in India today, let us see to it that there are ten tomorrow. But there are wrong as well as right ways of teaching science. A "superstition of facts" taught in the name of science were a poor exchange for a metaphysic, for a conviction of the subjectivity of all phenomena. In India, even the peasant will grant you that "All this is *Maya*"; he may not understand the full significance of what he says; but consider the deepening of European culture needed before the peasant there could say, however blindly, that "The world is but appearance, and by no means Thing-in-Itself".

[1] I describe the extreme product of English education, as seen for example, in Ceylon. Not all of these statements apply equally to every part of India. The remarks on dress and music are of universal application.

Secondly, the sacredness of all things—the antithesis of the European division of life into sacred and profane. The tendency in European religious development has been to exclude from the domain of religion every aspect of "worldly" activity. Science, art, sex, agriculture, commerce are regarded in the West as secular aspects of life, quite apart from religion. It is not surprising that under such conditions, those concerned with life in its reality, have come to feel the so-called religion that ignores the activities of life, as a thing apart, and of little interest or worth. In India, this was never so; religion idealizes and spiritualizes life itself, rather than excludes it. This intimate entwining of the transcendental and material, this annihilation of the possibility of profanity or vulgarity of thought, explains the strength and permanence of Indian faith, and demonstrates not merely the stupidity, but the wrongness of attempting to replace a religious culture by one entirely material.

Thirdly, the true spirit of religious toleration, illustrated continually in Indian history, and based upon a consciousness of the fact that all religious dogmas are formulas imposed upon the infinite by the limitations of the finite human intellect.

Fourthly, etiquette—civilization conceived of as the product of civil men. There is a Sinhalese proverb that runs, "Take the ploughman from the plough, and wash off his dirt, and he is fit to rule a kingdom." "This was spoken," says Knox, "of the people of Cande Uda (the highlands of Ceylon) because of the civility, understanding, and gravity of the poorest men among them. Their ordinary Plowmen and Husbandmen do speak elegantly, and are full of compliment. And there is no difference between the ability of speech of a Country man and a Courtier." There could be said of few people any greater things than these; but they cannot be said of those who have passed through the "instruction machines" of today; they belong to a society where life itself brought culture, not books alone.

Fifthly, special ideas in relation to education, such as the relation between teacher and pupil, implied in the words of *guru* and *chela* (master and disciple); memorizing great literature, the epics as embodying ideals of character; learning a privilege demanding qualifications, not to be forced on the unwilling or used as a mere road to material prosperity; extreme importance of the teacher's personality. "As the man who digs with a spade obtains water, even so an obedient (pupil) obtains the knowledge which lies in his teacher" (Manu II.218). This view is antithetic to the modern practice of making everything easy for the pupil.

Sixthly, the basis of ethics are not any commandments, but the principle of altruism, founded on the philosophical truth: "Thy neighbor is thyself." Recognition of the unity of all life.

Seventhly, control, not merely of action, but of thoughts; concentration, one-pointedness, capacity for stillness.

These are some of the points of view which are intrinsic in Indian culture, and must be recognized in any sound educational ideal for India; but are in the present system ignored or opposed. The aim should be to develop the people's intelligence through the medium of their own national culture. For the national culture is the only *Aussichtspunkt* [point of view] from which, in relation to a wider landscape, a man can rightly *sich am Denken orientiren* [orient himself in thinking]. To this culture has to be added, for those brought into contact with the modern idea, some part of that wider synthesis that should enable such a one to understand what may be the nature of the prospect seen from some other of the great headlands, the other national cultures, wherefrom humanity has gazed into the dim sea of the Infinite Unknown. To effect this wider synthesis, are needed signals and interpretations, rather than that laborious backward march through the emptiness of a spiritual desert where one may perish by the way, or if not so, then weary and footsore arrive at last upon one of those other headlands, only to learn, it may be, that there is to be found a less extensive prospect and a more barren soil. (5)

Our university must above all be a school of Oriental learning sufficient not only for ourselves, but to attract scholars from all parts of the world to learn the wisdom of the East in the East. (4)

The missionary must not be allowed to "educate," until he really understands the Indian people and desires to help them to solve their own problems in their own way; he must not be allowed to teach, until he himself has learnt. (64)

Alas for wasted opportunity! To share in the true education of the Indian woman were indeed a privilege. Behind her are the traditions of the great women of Indian history and myth, women strong in love and war, sainthood, in submission and in learning. She is still a guarded flame, this daughter of a hundred earls. She has not to struggle for a living in a competitive society, but is free to be herself. Upon her might be lavished the resources of all culture, to make yet more perfect that which is already most exquisitely so. You that have entered on the task so confidently, with the ulterior motive of conversion, have proved yourselves unfit. Lay no blame on India for her slowness to accept the education you have offered to her women; praise her rather for the wise instinct that leads her to mistrust you. When you learn that none can truly educate those against whose ideals they are blindly prejudiced; when you realize that you can but offer new modes of expression to faculties already exercised in other ways; when you come with reverence, as well to learn as to teach; when you establish schools within the Indian social ideal, and not antagonistic to it—then, perhaps, we may ask you to help us build upon that great foundation. Not I trust, before; lest there should be too much for the daughters of our daughters to unlearn. (5)

If the advocates of compulsory education were sincere, and by education meant education, they would be well aware that the first result of any real universal education would be to rear a race who would refuse point-blank the greater part of the activities offered by present-day civilized existence. I lay it at the door of science—not indeed as the prime cause, but as the immediate instrument—that life under Modern Western culture is not worth living, except for those who are strong enough and well enough equipped to maintain a perpetual guerilla warfare against all the purposes and idols of that civilization with a view to its utter transformation. (67)

IMPERIALISM & POLITICS

The beauty and logic of (Asiatic) Indian life belongs to a dying past, and the nineteenth century has degraded much and created nothing. If any blame for this is to be laid on alien shoulders, it should be only in the sense that if it must be that offences come, woe unto them through whom they come. It is an ungrateful and unromantic task to govern a subject race. England could not in any case have inspired a new life: the best she could have done would have been to understand and conserve through patronage and education the surviving categories of Indian civilization—architecture, music, handicrafts, popular and classic literature, and schools of philosophy—and that she failed here is to have been found wanting in imagination and sympathy. It should not have been regarded as the highest ideal of Empire "to give to all men an English mind." (3)

A nationalism which does not recognize the rights and duties of others but attempts to aggrandize itself at their expense, becomes no longer nationalism but a disease generally called Imperialism. (1)

It will never be possible for the European nationalist ideal that every nation should choose its own form of government, and lead its own life, to be realized—so long as the European nations have, or desire to have, possessions in Asia. What has to be secured is the common cooperation of East and West for common ends, not the subjugation of either to the other nor their lasting estrangement. (*)

The English-speaking peoples have, indeed labored under one great handicap, that of their domination by Rudyard Kipling, a skilled performer to the gallery, to be sure, but one whose irresponsible and uninstructured mentality represented all that an Englishman's ought never to have been. He, by giving free expression to his resentment of his own inability to synthesize the East and West in his own experience, has probably done more than any other one man to delay the recognition not alone of their ultimately common heritage, but even of their common humanity; more than any other Englishman to make it true for Englishmen that east of Suez "there ain't no Ten Commandments." You English-speaking peoples listened to him, nevertheless, and gave him a place in your literary pantheon where, in fact, he held up the mirror to the adolescent imperialistic mentality and carries its and his "white man's burden" so bravely. How can we think of you as grown-up men, as long as you play only with such toys as Kipling gave you, and only babble of green fields—the playing fields of Eton? It is high time that the Hollywood picture of India was forgotten. (38)

How many of our "communists," I wonder, realize that the reference of "the common Man," COMMUNIS HOMO, was originally not to the man in the street as such, but to the immanent deity, the very Man in everyman! (57)

A democracy is a government of all by a majority of proletarians; a Soviet, a government by a small group of proletarians; and a Dictatorship, a government by a single proletarian. In the traditional and unanimous society there is a government by an hereditary aristocracy, the function of which is to maintain an existing order, based on eternal principles, rather than to impose the views or arbitrary will (in the most technical sense of the words, a *tyrannical will*) of any "party" or "interest." (24)

Akbar Hands His Imperial Crown to Shah Jahan,
Mughal miniature, 1631

VOCATION

We need hardly say that from the traditional point of view there could hardly be found a stronger condemnation of the present social order than in the fact that the man at work is no longer doing what he likes best, but rather what he must, and in the general belief that a man can only be really happy when he "gets away" and is at play. For even if we mean by "happy" to enjoy the "higher things of life," it is a cruel error to pretend that this can be done at leisure if it has not been done at work. For "the man devoted to his own vocation finds perfection.... That man whose prayer and praise of God are in the doing of his own work perfects himself" (*Bhagavad Gita*). It is this way of life that our civilization denies to the vast majority of men, and in this respect that is notably inferior to even the most primitive or savage societies with which it can be contrasted. (21)

In an organized society it is every man's first duty to practice his own vocation; which inasmuch as vocation corresponds to nature, it is also his means of working out his own salvation; man's first duty socially thus coinciding with his first duty from the religious point of view. (77)

The *Bhagavad Gita* says, "Better one's own duty, though devoid of merit, than the duty of another well discharged." And this is the underlying theme of the whole Hindu social and religious structure. To the prince the duties of princehood are the one path of life; to the warrior the duties of his caste and vocation. The activities not ordained by caste and vocation are, however excellently performed, the gravest of sins and severely punishable by the state. (39)

It (caste) is the nearest approach that has yet been made towards a society where there shall be no attempt to realize a competitive equality, but where all interests are regarded as identical. (44)

The contentment of innumerable peoples can be destroyed in a generation by the withering touch of our civilization; the local market is flooded by a production in quantity with which the responsible maker by art cannot compete; the vocational structure of society, with all its guild organization and standards of workmanship, is undermined; the artist is robbed of his art and forced to find himself a "job"; until finally the ancient society is industrialized and reduced to the level of such societies as ours, in which business takes precedence of life. Can one wonder that Western nations are feared and hated by other peoples, not alone for obvious political or economic reasons, but even more profoundly and instinctively for spiritual reasons? (58)

The *Bhagavad Gita* in commending the caste system also speaks of the worker's "delight" in his work; the word employed, *abhi-rata* (*ram* with an intensifying prefix), might as well have been rendered by "being in love with," as if with a bride; a fundamental sense of the root is to "come to rest in," as desire comes to rest in its object, when this has been attained.... I have known hereditary craftsmen in Ceylon, carpenters and painters who regarded themselves as descendants of the archetypal All-worker (whose image they drew for me). At one time they were working for me at my own house, chiefly at the making of a painted chest for my own use.[1] They were to be paid at a day rate when the work was done; but far from trying to spin out the time, they were so much interested, so much involved in their work, that they insisted on being supplied with adequate light, so that they could go on working after dark.[2] There is your answer to the problem of overtime.[3] It is under these conditions, as Plato says, that "*more* will be done, and *better* done, and *more easily* than in any other way." (41)

Weavers in Tanjore, Tamil Nadu

[1] Now in the Colombo Museum.

[2] I once cited these facts in the course of a lecture given at one of our larger woman's colleges. I was informed that most of my audience found it almost incredible that men could thus ignore their own best economic interests; they could not imagine a willingness to work, unless for money.

[3] For those whose means of livelihood is also their natural vocation, the word has no meaning; their work is never done.

SWADESHI

True *swadeshi* ... is a way of looking at life. It is essentially sincerity. Seek first this, learn once more the art of living, and you will find that our ancient civilization, industrial no less than spiritual will re-arise from the ashes of our vulgarity and parasitism of today. (4)

True *swadeshi* would have attempted to preserve the status of our skilled artisans and village craftsmen, for the sake of the value to our country of men as Men. (4)

I have sought in vain for any expression in *swadeshi* writings of a primary desire to make goods more useful or more beautiful than those imported, or to preserve for the country any art, *qua* art, and not merely as an industry. (5)

Not infrequently the *swadeshi* cry is an exhortation to self-sacrifice. It seems to me that this is an entirely false position. It is never worthwhile in the long run putting up with second best. *Swadeshi* for the very poor may mean a real sacrifice of money. But how far this is really the case is very doubtful. If one should regard a standard of simple living conditioned by quality rather than quantity of wants, where durability of materials was preferred to cheapness alone, it is fairly certain that even the peasant would be better advised to use (real) *swadeshi* than foreign goods. And for those better off, for those who have adopted pseudo-European fashions and manners to talk of *swadeshi* as a sacrifice is cant of the worst description. It implies entire ignorance of India's achievement in the industrial arts, and an utter lack of faith in India. The blindest prejudice in favor of all things Indian were preferable to such condescension as that of one who casts aside the husks and trappings of modern luxury, to accept the mother's exquisite gifts as a "sacrifice." (5)

Not till the Indian people patronize Indian arts and industries from a real appreciation of them, and because they recognize them not merely as cheaper, but as better than the foreign, will the *swadeshi* movement become complete and comprehensive. If a time should ever come—and at present it seems far off—when Indians recognize that "for the beautification of an Indian house or the furniture of an Indian home there is no need to rush to European shops in Calcutta or Bombay," there may be a realization of *swadeshi*. But "so long as they prefer to fill their palaces with flaming Brussels carpets, Tottenham Court Road furniture, cheap Italian mosaics, French oleographs, Austrian lustres, German tissues and cheap brocades, there is not much hope." When will Indians make it impossible for any enemy to throw in their teeth a reproach so true as this?

Even more important, then, than the establishment of new industries on Indian soil, are the patronage and revival of those on the verge of extinction, the purification of those which survive in degraded forms, and the avoidance of useless luxuries, whether made in India or not. *Swadeshi* must be inspired by a broad and many-sided national sentiment, and must have definitely constructive aims; where such a sentiment exists, industrial *swadeshi* will be its inevitable outcome without effort and without failure. (5)

This is not civilization; this is not the art of living. Civilization consists, not in multiplying our desires and the means of gratifying them, but in the refinement of their quality. Industry per se, is no advantage. The true end of material civilization is not production, but use; not labor, but leisure; not to destroy, but to make possible, spiritual culture. A nation which sees its goal rather in the production of things than in the lives of men must in the end deservedly perish. Therefore it is that the *swadeshi* movement, a synthesis of effort for the regeneration of India, should be guided by that true political economy that seeks to make men wise and happy, rather than merely to multiply their goods at the cost of physical and spiritual degradation. (5)

It is suicidal to compete with European basis of cheapness. Competition should be on the basis of quality. (4)

Learn not to waste the vital forces of the nation in a temporary political conflict but understand that art will enable you to reestablish all your arts and industries on a surer basis. *Swadeshi* must be something more than a political weapon. It must be a religious artistic ideal. (4)

In exchange for this world of beauty that was our birthright, the nineteenth century has made our country a "dumping ground" for all the vulgar superfluities of European over-production. (4)

Think of our duty from another point of view; is not the ancient virtue of hospitality binding on us? Yet now the shame of hospitality refused is ours; how many have come to India, reverencing her past, ready to learn of her still, and have been sent empty away! The student of Social Economy finds a highly organized society in the process of disintegration without any of the serious and constructive effort required for its reorganization under changed conditions; the student of Architecture finds a tradition living still, but scorned by a people devoted to the imitation of their rulers, building copies of English palaces and French villas in the very presence of men who still know how to build, and under the shadow of buildings as noble as any that the world has seen. The student of Fine Arts is shown inferior imitations of the latest European "styles," where he should find some new and living revelation; the decorative artist sees the traditional craftsmen of India thrown out of employment by the mechanical vulgarities of Birmingham and Manchester, without the least effort made to preserve for future generations the accumulated skill and cunning of centuries of the manufacture of materials and wares which have commanded the admiration of the world. The musician of other lands hears little but the gramophone or the harmonium in India; the man of religion finds the crudest materialism replacing a reasoned metaphysic; the lover of freedom beholds a people who can be imprisoned or deported for indefinite periods without trial, and too divided amongst themselves to offer adequate resistance to this lawlessness; in a word, every man seeking to widen his own outlook, sees but his own face distorted in an Indian mirror. (5)

INDIAN WOMEN

It would have been contrary to the spirit of Indian culture to deny to individual women the opportunity of saintship or learning in the sense of closing to them the schools of divinity or science after the fashion of the Western academies in the nineteenth century. But where the social norm is found in marriage and parenthood for men and women alike, it could only have been in exceptional cases and under exceptional circumstances that the latter specialized, whether in divinity, like Auvvai, Mira Bai, or the Buddhist nuns, in science, like Lilavati, or in war, like Chand Bibi or the Rani of Jhansi. Those set free to cultivate expert knowledge of science or to follow with undivided allegiance either religion or any art, could only be *sannyasini* or devotee, the widow, and the courtesan. A majority of women have always, and naturally, preferred marriage and motherhood to either of these conditions. But those who felt the call of religion, those from whom a husband's death removed the central motif of their life, and those trained from childhood as expert artists, have always maintained a great tradition in various branches of cultural activity, such as social service or music. What we have to observe is that Hindu sociologists have always regarded these specializations as more or less incompatible with wifehood and motherhood; life is not long enough for the achievement of many different things. (3)

Detail of a painting from the *Bahari Sat Sai*, Kangra, 18th century

Western critics have often asserted that the Oriental woman is a slave, and that we have made her what she is. We can only reply that we do not identify freedom with self-assertion, and that the Oriental woman is what she is, only because our social and religious culture has permitted her to be and to remain essentially feminine.

Exquisite as she may be in literature and art we dare not claim for ourselves as men the whole honor of creating such a type, however persistently the industrious industrial critic would thrust upon us.

The Eastern woman is not, at least we do not claim that she is, superior to other women in her innermost nature; she is perhaps an older, purer, and more specialized type, but certainly a universal type, and it is precisely here that the industrial woman departs from type. Nobility in a woman does not depend upon race, but upon ideals; it is the outcome of a certain view of life.

Savitri, Padmavati, Sita, Radha, Uma, Lilavati, Tara—our divine and human heroines—have a universal fellowship, for everything feminine is of the Mother. Who could have been more wholly devoted than Alcetis, more patient than Griselda, more loving than Deirdre, more a soldier than Joan of Arc, more Amazon than Brynhild? (3)

Even in recent times, in families where the men have received an English education unrelated to Indian life and thought, the inheritance of Indian modes of thought and feeling rests in the main with women; for a definite philosophy of life is bound up with household ritual and traditional etiquette and finds expression equally in folk-tale and cradle song and popular poetry, and in those Puranic and epic songs which constitute the household Bible literature of India. Under these conditions it is often the case that Indian women, with all their faults of sentimentality and ignorance, have remained the guardians of a spiritual culture which is of greater worth than the efficiency and information of the educated. (3)

No story is more appropriate than that of Madalasa and her son Vikranta to illustrate the position of the Indian mother as teacher. As Vikranta grew up day by day, the *Markandeya Purana* relates, Madalasa "taught him knowledge of the Self by ministering to him in sickness; and as he grew in strength and there waxed in him his father's heart, he attained to knowledge of the Self by his mother's words." And these were Madalasa's words, spoken to the baby crying on her lap: "My child, thou art without a name or form, and it is but in fantasy that thou hast been given a name. This thy body, framed of the five elements, is not thine in sooth, nor art thou of it. Why does thou weep? Or, maybe, thou weepest not; it is a sound self-born that

Left: Sita; *Center*: Uma; *Right*: Parvati

cometh forth from the king's son.... In the body dwells another self, and therewith abideth not the thought that 'This is mine,' which appertaineth to the flesh. Shame that man is so deceived!" (3)

It is not, indeed, by contrasting the religious standpoints of the East and the West that the supposed inferior position of woman in the East can be demonstrated. At the present day there are millions of Orientals who worship the Divine life in the image of a woman. Woman is honored in religious literature and art.

Mahadev, addressing Uma, in the *Mahabharata* says, "Thou O Lady, knowest both the Self and the Not-Self.... Thou art skilled in every work. Thou art endured with self-restraint and with perfect same-sightness in respect of every creature. Thy energy and power are equal to My own, and Thou hast not shrunk from the most severe austerities."

Again, the *Ramayana*, when Rama leaves his kingdom to live as a hermit in the forest, Vasishtha, pleading that Sita should not follow him, suggests that she should reign in his stead: "Sita will occupy Rama's seat. Of all these that marry, the wife is the soul. Sita will govern the earth, as she is Rama's self." Sita, however chooses to follow Rama.

In the great law book of Manu we find: "Where women are honored, there the gods are pleased; but where they are not honored no sacred rite yields rewards." There is too, the Indian saying: "Thou shall not strike a woman even with a flower."

In Sufi mysticism, the Beloved (feminine) is "all that lives"—God: the Lover (masculine), is a "dead thing"—the individual so lacking the Divine Life. These lines were written by Jalaluddin Rumi:

Woman is a ray of God, not a mere mistress.
The Creator's Self, as it were, not a mere creature! (46)

I would admit women to absolute equality of opportunity with men in all respects. But I think that State most fortunate wherein most women between the ages of twenty and forty are primarily concerned with the making of children, beautiful in every sense. To this end women must obtain economic security, either from individuals or from the State. There can be no freedom for women which does not include the freedom to have, as well as not to have children. It is ultimately I conceive—at least, I hope—for the right to be themselves, rather than for the right to become more like men, that Suffragettes are, however unconsciously, fighting. There can be no freedom for women till good motherhood is regarded as an intrinsic glory. (46)

The infant Krishna with her foster mother Yasoda, Tamil Nadu, 12th century

The East has always recognized the fundamental difference in the psychology of men and women. I do not think that any attempt to minimize or to ignore differences can be successful. It is because men and women are different that they need each other. What is needed at present is that women should be allowed to discover for themselves what is their "sphere," rather than that they should continue to occupy perforce the sphere which men (rightly or wrongly) have at various times allowed to them in the patriarchal ages. This necessity is as much a necessity for the West as for the East.

Social status, as I have said, needs reformation both in the East and in the West. But the West far more than the East needs a change of heart. The Western view of sex is degraded and materially contrasted with the Eastern. Women are not lightly spoken of, or written of, in the East as they are so often in the West. Sex for the Oriental is a sacrament. For the European it is a pleasure.

With the consciousness of this, and much more that might be added to it, I feel that the West has at least as much to learn from the East of reverence to women as the East has to learn from the West. And it is better for reformers, whether in the East or West, to work together for a common end than to pride themselves upon their own supposedly superior achievement. (46)

Why should women have sought for modes of self-advertisement that held no lure even for men? The governing concept of Hindu ethics is vocation (*dharma*); the highest merit consists in the fulfillment of "one's own duty," in other words, in dedication to one's calling. Hindu society was highly organized; and where it was considered wrong for a man to fulfill the duties of another man rather than his own, how much more must a confusion of function as between woman and man have seemed wrong, where differentiation is so much more evident. In the words of Manu: "To be mothers were women created, and to be fathers men"; and adds significantly, "therefore are religious sacraments ordained in the *Veda* to be observed by the husband together with the wife." (3)

It is sometimes asked, what opportunities are open to the Oriental woman? How can she express herself? The answer is that life is so designed that she is given the opportunity to be a woman—in other words, to realize, rather than to express, herself. It is possible that modern Europe errs in the opposite direction. We must also remember that very much which passes for education nowadays is superficial; some of it amounts to little more than parlor tricks, and nothing is gained by communicating this condition to Asia, where I have heard of modern parents who desired that their

Young Lady Beneath a Tree, Mughal painting

daughters should be taught "a little French" or "a few strokes on the violin." The arts in India are professional, vocational, demanding undivided service; nothing is taught to the amateur by way of social accomplishment or studied superficially. And woman represents the continuity of the racial life, an energy which cannot be divided or diverted without a corresponding loss of racial vitality; she can no more desire to be something other than herself, than the *vaishya* could wish to be known as a *kshatriya*, or the *kshatriya*, as a *brahman*. (3)

I doubt if anyone will deny that it is the function or nature of women, as a group—not necessarily in every individual case—in general, to be mothers, alike in spiritual and physical senses. What we have to do then, is not to assert the liberty of women to deny the duty or right of motherhood, however we regard it, but to accord this function a higher protection and honor than it now receives. And here, perhaps, there is still something to be learnt in Asia. There the pregnant woman is auspicious, and receives the highest respect; whereas in many industrial and secular Western societies she is an object of more or less open ridicule, she is ashamed to be seen abroad, and tries to conceal her condition, sometimes even by means that are injurious to her own and the child's health. That this was not the case in a more vital period of European civilization may be seen in all the literature and art of the Middle Ages and particularly in the status of the Virgin Mary, whose motherhood endeared her to the folk so much more than her virginity. (3)

To avoid misunderstanding, let me say in passing, that in depicting the life of Hindu women as fulfilling a great ideal, I do not mean to indicate the Hindu social formula as a thing to be repeated or imitated. This would be a view as futile as that of the Gothic revival in architecture; the reproduction of period furniture does not belong to life. A perfection that has been can never be a perfection for us. (3)

Rajput drawing from Jaipur

MARRIAGE

Thus in Hindu society the social order is placed before the happiness of the individual, whether man or woman. This is the explanation of the greater peace which distinguishes the arranged marriage of the East; where there is no deception there can be no disappointment. And since the conditions on which it is founded do not change, it is logical that Hindu marriage should be indissoluble; only when social duties have been fulfilled and social debts paid, is it permissible for the householder to relinquish simultaneously the duties and the rights of the social individual. It is also logical that when the marriage is childless it is permissible to take a second wife with the consent—and often at the wish—of the first. (3)

The Asiatic theory of marriage, which would have been perfectly comprehensible in the Middle Ages, before the European woman had become an economic parasite, and which is still very little removed from that of Roman or Greek Christianity, is not readily intelligible to the industrial democratic consciousness of Europe and America, which is so much more concerned for rights than for duties, and desires more than anything else to be released from responsibilities—regarding such release as freedom. (3)

It is thus that Western reformers would awaken a divine discontent in the hearts of Oriental women, forgetting that the way of ego-assertion cannot be a royal road to realization of the Self. The industrial mind is primarily sentimental, and therefore cannot reason clearly upon love and marriage; but the Asiatic analysis is philosophic, religious, and practical. (3)

Hinduism justifies no cult of ego-expression, but aims consistently at spiritual freedom. Those who are conscious of a sufficient inner life become the more indifferent to outward expression of their own or any changing personality. The ultimate purposes of Hindu social discipline are that men should unify their individuality with a wider and deeper than individual life, should fulfill appointed tasks regardless of failure or success, distinguish the timeless from its shifting forms, and escape the all-too-narrow prison of the "I and mine." (3)

Current Western theory seeks to establish marriage on a basis of romantic love and free choice; marriage thus depends on the accident of "falling in love." Those who are "crossed in love" or do not love are not required to marry. This individualistic position, however, is only logically defensible if at the same time it is recognized that to fall out of love must end the marriage. It is a high and religious ideal which justifies sexual relations only as the outward expression demanded by passionate love and regards an intimacy continued or begun for mere pleasure, or for reasons of prudence, or even as a duty, as essentially immoral; it is an ideal which isolated individuals and groups have constantly upheld; and it may be that the ultimate development of idealistic individualism will tend to a nearer realization of it. (3)

But do not let us deceive ourselves that because the Western marriage is nominally founded upon free choice, it therefore secures a permanent unity of spiritual and physical passion. On the contrary, perhaps in a majority of cases, it holds together those who are no longer "in love"; habit, considerations of prudence, or, if there are children, a sense of duty often compel the passionless continuance of a marriage for the initiation of which romantic love was felt to be a *sine qua non*. Those who now live side by side upon a basis of affection and common interest would not have entered upon marriage on this basis alone. (3)

If the home is worth preserving under modern conditions—and in India at any rate, the family is still the central element of social organization—, then probably the "best solution" will always be found in some such compromise as is implied in a more or less permanent marriage; though greater tolerance than is now usual must be accorded to exceptions above and below the norm. What are we going to regard as the constructive basis of the normal marriage? (3)

For Hindu sociologists marriage is a social and ethical relationship, and the begetting of children the payment of a debt. Romantic love is a brief experience of timeless freedom, essentially religious and ecstatic, in itself as purely anti-social as every glimpse of Union is a denial of the Relative; it is the way of Mary. It is true the glamor of this experience may persist for weeks and months, when the whole of life is illuminated by the partial merging of the consciousness of the lover and beloved; but sooner or later in almost every case there must follow a return to the world of unreality, and that insight which once endowed the beloved with innumerable perfections fades in the light of common sense. The lovers are fortunate if there remains to them a basis of common interest and common duty and a mutuality of temperament adequate for friendship, affection, and forbearance; upon this chance depends the possibility of happiness during the greater part of almost every married life. (3)

The Hindu marriage differs from the marriage of sentiment mainly in putting these considerations first. Here, as elsewhere, happiness will arise from the fulfillment of vocation, far more than when immediate satisfaction is made the primary end. I use the term vocation advisedly; for the Oriental marriage, like the Oriental actor's art, is the fulfillment of a traditional design, and does not depend upon the accidents of sensibility. To be such a man as Rama, such a wife as Sita, rather than to express "oneself," is the aim. The formula is predetermined; husband and wife alike have parts to play; and it is from this point of view that we can best understand the meaning of Manu's law, that a wife should look on her husband as a god, regardless of his personal merit or demerits—it would be beneath her dignity to deviate from a woman's norm merely because of the failure of a man. It is for her own sake and for the sake of the community, rather than for his alone, that life must be attuned to the eternal unity of *Purusa* and *Prakriti*. (3)

Sita, Rama, and Lakhsmana, Kangra, c. 1780

2. ART

While the Clouds Gather, Kangra, 19th century

ART

"Art is expression" (Croce): "Art (*kavya*) is a statement informed by *rasa*" (*Sahityadarpana*): art is man's handiwork. Art is fine or beautiful to the degree in which it is done finely and achieves its proper intentions; it is not art or ugly to the degree in which it is done carelessly and fails to achieve its proper intentions. These intentions are always the satisfaction of human necessities, which necessities are never purely practical (physical) nor purely theoretical (spiritual); man needs bread, but does not live by bread alone. When these necessities are purely individual, art is isolated from its environment and requires explanation even to contemporaries, and it is difficult to see why such art should be exhibited. When these necessities are general (e.g. early Italian painting or Indian sculpture), art is comprehensible to all normal contemporaries, and is used rather than exhibited. The latter kind of art may even become "universal," i.e. comprehensible and serviceable beyond its original environment. (44)

Art is a language, and will be a dead language if no change in it be permitted; if it is not to be a medium of expression of new ideas and new thoughts, it will lose relatively to the national life. But like the spoken language it can only change nobly, in response to an impulse from within, the irresistible demand for words, in which to communicate the new (emotions) conceptions. The aims of the Indian art are not for one time only; the synthesis of Indian thought is one whole (compound) composed equally of present, past, and future. We stand in relation to both; the past has made us what we are, the future we ourselves are molding; our duty to the future is to enrich, not to destroy the past. The aim and the method are eternal. The formula and the vision must change and widen. The future is to be greater than the past; not contemptuous of it; but its inevitable product, an integral part of it. (23)

It is not to enlarge our collection of bric-a-brac that we ought to study ancient or foreign arts, but to enlarge our own consciousness of being. (8)

The true critic, *rasika*, perceives the beauty of which the artist has exhibited the signs. (3)

The poet is born, not made; but so also is the *rasika* whose genius differs in degree, not in kind, from that of the original artist. (3)

It is of the essence of art to bring back into order the multiplicity of Nature, and it is in this sense that it "prepares all creatures to return to God." Decadent art is simply an art that is no longer felt or energized. (*)

Modern European art endeavors to represent things as they are in themselves, Asiatic and Christian art to represent things as they are in God, or nearer to their source. (24)

If bees have been deceived by painted flowers, why was honey not provided?... The more an image is true to nature, the more it lies. (30)

Mere narration (*nirvaha*, *itihasa*), bare utility, are not art, or are only art in a rudimentary sense. Only the man of little wit can fail to recognize that art, by nature, is a well-spring of delight, whatever may have been the occasion of its appearance. On the other hand, there cannot be imagined an art without meaning or use. The doctrine of art for art's sake is disposed of in a sentence quoted in the *Sahitya Darpana*, V.L. Commentary: "All expression (*vakya*), human or revealed, are directed to an end beyond themselves (*haryaparam*) or if not so determined (*ata-partve*) are thereby comparable only to the utterances of a madman." (30)

Anonymity is thus in accordance with the truth; and it is one of the proudest distinctions of the Hindu culture. The names of the "authors" of the epics are but shadows, and in later ages it was a constant practice of writers to suppress their own names and ascribe their work to a mythical or famous poet, thereby to gain a better attention for the truth that they would rather claim to have "heard" than to have "made." Similarly, scarcely a single Hindu painter or sculptor is known by name; and the entire range of Sanskrit literature cannot exhibit a single autobiography and but little history. (3)

What we mean by "original" is "coming from its source within" like water from a spring.... There can be no property in ideas. The individual does not make them, but *finds them*; let him only see to it that he really takes possession of them, and work will be original in the same sense that the recurrent seasons, sunrise and sunset are ever new although in name the same. (45)

The absence of names in the history of Indian art is a great advantage to the historian of art, for he is forced to concentrate all his attention upon their work, and its reaction to life and thought as a whole, while all temptation to anecdotal criticism is removed. (6)

The Indian artist, although a person, is not a personality; his personal

Krishna and the Gopis, Kangra, 19th century

idiosyncrasy is at the most a part of his equipment, and never the occasion of his art. All of the greatest Indian works are anonymous, and all that we know of the lives of Indian artists in any field could be printed in a tract of a dozen pages. (8)

Nations are created by artists and poets, not by merchants and politicians. In art lies the deepest life principles. (5)

To the "primitive" man who, like the angels, had fewer ideas and used less means than we, it had been inconceivable that anything, whether natural or artificial, could have a use or value only and not also a meaning; this man literally could not have understood our distinction of sacred from profane or of spiritual from material values; he did not live by bread alone. It had not occurred to him that there could be such a thing as an industry without art, or the practice of any art that was not at the same time a ritual going on with what had been done by God in the beginning. (24)

The representation of a man must really correspond to the idea of the man, but must not look so like him as to deceive the eye; for the work of art is a mind-made thing and aims at the mind, but an illusion is no more *intelligible* than the natural object it mimics. (That, I think, settles the whole question of naturalism.) (24)

We ought then, to appreciate Indian art from every point of view, to be equipped with learning, piety, sensibility, knowledge of technique, and simplicity, combining the qualities of the *pandita*, the *bhakta*, the *acarya*, and the *alpa-buddhi jana.* (37)

The Indian must see with his own eye. Two things are needful; one that he should be saturated with the traditional art of his race in order that he may know how to see; the other, that he be saturated with the traditional culture of the East that he may know what to see. (*)

Try to believe in the regeneration of India through art, and not by politics and economics alone. A purely material ideal will never give to us the lacking strength to build up a great enduring nation. For that we need ideals and dreams impossible and visionary, the food of martyrs and of artists. (76)

The Hindus have never believed in art for art's sake; their art, like that of medieval Europe, was an art for love's sake. (6)

In the first place all Hindu art (Brahmanical and *Mahayana* Buddhist) is religious. (6)

We ought not, then, to like a work of art merely because it is like something we like. It is unworthy to exploit a picture or a phrase merely as a

A potter in Ceylon

substitute for a beautiful environment or a beloved friend. We ought not to demand to be pleased and flattered, for our true need is to be touched by love or fear. The meaning of art is far deeper than that of its immediate subject. (6)

What is art, or rather what was art? In the first place the property of the artist, a kind of knowledge and skill by which he knows not what ought to be made, but how to imagine the form of the things that is to be made, and how to embody this form in suitable material, so that the resulting artifact may be used. The ship-builder builds, not for aesthetic reasons, but in order that men may be able to sail on the water; it is a matter of fact that the well-built ship will be beautiful, but it is not for the sake of making something beautiful that the ship-builder goes to work; it is a matter of fact that a well made icon will be beautiful, in other words, that it will please when seen by those for whose use it was made, but the imager is casting his bronze primarily for use and not as a mantelpiece ornament or for the museum showcase. (22)

I do not perceive a fundamental distinction of arts as national—Indian, Greek, or English. All art interprets life; it is like the *Veda*s, eternal, independent of the accidental conditions of those who see or hear. (6)

Art is not an aesthetic but a rhetorical activity. (*)

Indian art and culture was a joint creation of the Dravidian and Aryan genius, a welding together of symbolic and representative, abstract and explicit, language and thought. (2)

We are peculiar people. I say this with reference to the fact that whereas almost all other peoples have called their theory of art or expression a "Rhetoric" and have thought of art as a kind of knowledge, we have invented an "Aesthetic" and think of art as a kind of feeling.

The Greek original of the word "aesthetic" means "perception by the senses, especially by feeling." (24).

Art contains in itself the deepest principles of life, the truest guide to the greatest art, the Art of Living. The true life, the ideal of Indian culture, is itself a unity and an art, because of its inspiration by one ruling passion, the desire to realize a spiritual inheritance. All things in India have been valued in the light of this desire. (*)

The artist is not a special kind of man, but every man who is not an artist in some field, every man without a vocation, is an idler. The kind of artist that a man should be, carpenter, painter, lawyer, farmer, or priest, is determined by his own nature, in other words by his nativity. The only man who has a right to abstain from all constructive activities is the monk, who has also surrendered all those uses that depend on things that can be made and is no longer a member of society. No man has a right to any social status, who is not an artist. (16)

The anonymity of the artist belongs to a type of culture dominated by the longing to be liberated from oneself. All the force of this philosophy is directed against the delusion "I am the doer." "I" am not in fact the doer, but the instrument; human individuality is not an end but only a means. The supreme achievement of individual consciousness is to lose or find (both words mean the same) itself in what is both its first beginning and its last end. All that is required of the instrument is efficiency and obedience; it is not for the subject to aspire to the throne; the constitution of man is not a democracy, but the hierarchy of body, soul, and spirit. Is it for the Christian to consider any work "his own," when even Christ has said that "I do nothing of myself"? Or for the Hindu, when Krishna has said, "The comprehensor cannot form the concept 'I am the doer'"? Or for the Buddhist, for whom it has been said that "To wish that it may be made known that 'I was the author' is the thought of a man not yet adult"? (16)

It cannot be too clearly understood that the mere representation of nature is never the aim of Indian art. Probably no truly Indian sculpture has been wrought from a living model or any religious painting copied from life. Possibly no Hindu artist of the old schools ever drew from nature at all. His store of memory pictures, his power of visualization and his imagination were for his purpose finer means, for he desired to suggest the Idea behind sensuous appearance not to give the detail of seeming reality that was in truth but *Maya*, illusion.... To mistake *Maya* for reality were error indeed. "Men of no understanding think of Me, the unmanifest, as having manifestation, knowing not My higher being to be Changeless, Supreme" (*Bhagavad Gita* VII, 24). (27)

The particular form suitable to each image is to be found described in the *Shilpa Shastras*, the canonical texts followed by the image-makers.... These texts supply the data needed for the mental representation which serves as the sculptor's model. According to his vision, says Shukracharya, he will fashion in temples the image of the divinities he adores. It is thus, and not by some other means, in truth and not by direct observation, that he will be able to attain his goal. —The essential part of art, the "visualization" (and one could say the same of the ecstatic audition of the musician) is thus a kind of *yoga*; the artist is sometimes looked on as a sort of *yogi*.

Often, before undertaking his work, he celebrates certain special rites aimed at stifling the working of the conscious will and setting free the subjective faculties. In this case truth does not come from visual observation but from "muscular awareness" of the movements the artist has understood and realized in his own members. —The *Shastras* also give the canons of proportion. These proportions vary according to the divinity to be represented. Architecture also has its own canons which regulate even the very smallest details. (86)

Great art or science is the flower of a free national life pouring its abundant energy into ever new channels, giving some new intimation of a truth and harmony before unknown or forgotten. (5)

Partial view of the Meenakshi Temple at Madurai, Tamil Nadu

There is a close affinity between art and religion which is seldom understood, and we very often overlook the fact that aesthetic and religious spheres exhibit a natural kinship. (30)

Nothing is common or unclean. All life is a sacrament, no part of it more so than another, and there is no part of it that may not symbolize eternal and infinite things. In this great same-sightedness the opportunity for art is great. But in this religious art it must not be forgotten that life is not to be represented for its own sake but for the sake of the Divine expressed in and through it. (5)

It is hardly necessary to point out that the Vedic sacrifice, which is always described as the imitation of "what was at the beginning," is, in all its forms and in the full meaning of the terms, a work of art and at the same time a synthesis of the arts of liturgy and architecture, and one can say the same of the Christian Mass (which is also a sacrifice in mime) where the dramatic and architectural elements are inseparably united. (87)

Art is the endeavor to transcend the duality of subject and object by the subjectification of nature and objectification of spirit. Religion is the endeavor to live with the Divine as own with own, as lovers with beloved. (30)

Thus during many centuries the artists of one district apply themselves to the interpretation of the same ideas; the origin of those ideas is more remote than any particular example. The great types are the fruit of communal rather than individual thought. This communal thought however is not only popular thought but that of the greatest and wisest minds of successive generations seeking to impress their vision on a whole race. (6)

In almost every art and craft, as also in music, there exists in Hindustan a complete and friendly fusion of the two cultures. The non-sectarian character of the styles of Indian art has indeed always been conspicuous; so that it is often only by special details that one can distinguish Jain from Buddhist *stupas*, Buddhist from Hindu sculpture, or the Hindu from the Musulman minor crafts. The one great distinction of Mughal from Hindu art is not so much racial as social; the former is an art of courts and connoisseurs, owing much to individual patronage, the latter belongs as much to the folk as to the kings. (6)

I should like to point out that "art" is like "God," precisely in this respect, that it cannot be seen; all that we can see is *things made by art*, and hence properly called artifacts, and these are analogous to those effects, which are all that we can see of God. The art remains in the artist, regardless of the vicissitudes to which his works are subject; and I protest against the serious use of the term "art" by a writer who really means "works of art." (66)

Let us then admit that the greater part of what is taught in the fine arts department of our universities, all of the psychologies of art, all the obscurities of modern aesthetics, are only so much verbiage, only a kind of defence that stands in the way of our understanding of the wholesome art, at the same time iconographically true and practically useful, that was once to be had in the marketplace or from any good artist.... Our aesthetic is nothing but a false rhetoric, and a flattery of human weakness by which we can account only for the arts that have no other purpose than to please. (24)

Things made by art answer to human needs, or else are luxuries. Human needs are the needs of the whole man, who does not live by bread alone. That means that to tolerate insignificant, i.e. meaningless conveniences, however convenient they may be, is beneath our natural dignity; the whole man needs things well and truly made to serve at one and the same time the needs of the active and contemplative life. On the other hand, pleasure taken in things well made is not a need in us independent of our need for the things themselves, but a part of our very nature; pleasure perfects the operation, but is not its end; the purposes of art are wholly utilitarian, in the full sense of the word as it applies to the whole man. We cannot give the name of art to anything irrational. (73)

Just as we desire peace but not the things that make for peace, so we desire art but not the things that make for art. (24)

Our artists are "emancipated" from any obligation to eternal verities, and have abandoned to tradesmen the satisfaction of present needs. Our abstract art is not an iconography of transcendental forms but the realistic picture of a disintegrated mentality. (85)

Our "aesthetic" approach can be compared only to that of a traveler who, when he sees a signpost, proceeds to admire its elegance, asks who made it, and finally cuts it down and takes it home to be used as a mantelpiece ornament. (88)

Detail of inlaid decoration in the Taj Mahal

BEAUTY

Beauty is not in any special or exclusive sense a property of works of art, but much rather a quality or value that may be manifested by all things that are, in proportion to the degree of their actual being and perfection. Beauty may be recognized either in spiritual or material substances, and if in the latter then either in natural objects or in works of art. Its conditions are always the same. (24)

The traditional doctrine of beauty is not developed with respect to artifacts alone, but universally. It is independent of taste. The recognition of beauty depends on judgment, not on sensation; the beauty of the aesthetic surfaces depends on their information, and not upon themselves. The work of art is beautiful, in terms of perfection, or truth and aptitude. Beauty is perfection apprehended as an attractive power; that aspect of the truth, which moves the will to grapple with the theme to be communicated. (58)

The quality of beauty in a work of art is quite independent of its theme. (3)

There are no degrees of beauty: the most complex and the simplest expression remind us of one and the same state. The sonata cannot be more beautiful than the simplest lyric, nor the painting than the drawing merely because of their greater elaboration. A mathematical analogy is found if we consider large and small circles; these differ only in their content, not in their circularity. (3)

As there are two Truths, absolute and relative (*vidaya* and *avidya*), so there are two Beauties, the one absolute or ideal, the other relative and better termed loveliness, because determined by human affections. These two are clearly distinguished in Indian aesthetics. (54)

The vision of beauty is thus an act of pure contemplation, not in the absence of any object of contemplation, but in conscious identification with the object of contemplation. (51)

The vision of beauty is spontaneous, in just the same sense as the inward light of the lover (*bhakta*). It is a state of grace that cannot be achieved by deliberate effort; though perhaps we can remove hindrances to its manifestation, for there are many witnesses that the secret of all art is to be found in self-forgetfulness. And we know that this state of grace is not achieved in the

The Bath, Kangra, 18th century

pursuit of pleasure; the hedonists have their reward, but they are in bondage to loveliness, while the artist is free in beauty. (3)

Hindu writers say that the capacity to feel beauty (to taste *rasa*) cannot be acquired by study, but is the reward of merit gained in a past life; for many good men and would-be historians of art have never perceived it. (3)

Rasa is not an objective quality in art, but a spiritual activity or experience called "tasting" (*asvada*)... arising from a perfected self-identification with the theme, whatever it may have been. This pure and disinterested aesthetic experience, indistinguishable from knowledge of the impersonal *Brahman*, impossible to be described otherwise than an intellectual ecstasy, can be evoked only in the spectator possessing the necessary competence, an inward criterion of truth (*pramana*). (54)

Possessions are a necessity to the extent that we can use them: it is altogether legitimate to enjoy what we do use, but equally inordinate to enjoy what we cannot use or to use what cannot be enjoyed. All possessions not at the same time beautiful and useful are an affront to human dignity. Ours is perhaps the first society to find it natural that some things should be beautiful and others useful. To be voluntarily poor is to have rejected what we cannot both admire and use: this definition can be applied alike to the case of the millionaire and to that of the monk. (21)

The Radiant Beauty, Kangra, 18th century

Mithuna (lovers), carved figures from Khajuraho, Madhya Pradesh, 11th century

EROS

In India we could not escape the conviction that sexual love has a deep and spiritual significance. There is nothing with which we can better compare the "mystic union" of the finite with its infinite ambient—that one experience which proves itself and is the only ground of faith—than the self-oblivion of earthly lovers locked in each other's arms, where "each is both." Physical proximity, contact, and interpenetration are the expressions of love, only because love is the recognition of identity. These two are one flesh, because they have remembered their unity of spirit. This is moreover a fuller identity than the mere sympathy of two individuals, and each as individual has now no more significance for the other than the gates of heaven for one who stands within. It is like an algebraic equation where the equation is the only truth and the terms may stand for anything. The least intrusion of the ego, however, involves a return to the illusion of duality. (3)

In the language of human love the Vaisnava mystics found ready to their hands a most explicit vocabulary of devotion and of union. The ultimate essential of all such devotion is self-forgetfulness and self-surrender, the root of all division is pride and self-will, and therefore the drama of spiritual experience is represented by the love of woman for man. (78)

There is also a great difference between the Eastern and Western attitude towards sexual intercourse; on the one hand the ethic of Hinduism, with its ideals of renunciation, is even severer than that of Roman Catholic Christianity; on the other we have to note that Hinduism embraces and recognizes and idealizes the whole of life. Thus it is that sex relation can be treated frankly and simply in religious and poetic literature and art. In its highest form, the sex relation is a sacrament and even more secularly regarded, it is rather an art than a mere animal gratification. (53)

Indian sex-symbolism assumes two main forms, the recognition of which will assist the student of art; first, the desire and union of individuals, sacramental in its likeness to the union of the individual soul with God. This is the love of the herd-girls for Krishna; and second, the creation of the world, manifestation, *Lila*, as the fruit of the union of male and female cosmic principles—*Purusa* and *Sakti*. (6)

Krishna and Radha, Kangra, 18th century

The two (lovers) are one flesh because they have remembered their unity of spirit. (*)

There is scarcely a single female figure represented in early Indian art without erotic suggestion on some kink, implied or explicitly expressed and emphasized. (*)

The mysticism of oriental art is always expressed in definite forms. India is wont to suggest the eternal and inexpressible infinities in terms of sensuous beauty. The love of man for woman or for nature are one with his love for God. (49)

In nearly all Indian art there runs a vein of deep sex-mysticism; not merely are female forms felt to be equally appropriate with male to adumbrate the majesty of the over-soul, but the interplay of all psychic and sexual forces is felt in itself to be religious. Here is no thought that passion is degrading but a frank recognition of the close analogy between amorous and religious ecstasy. It is thus that the imager, speaking always for the race rather than of personal idiosyncrasies, set side by side on his cathedral walls the *yogi* and the *apsara*, the saint and the ideal courtesan; accepting life as he saw it, he interpreted all its phenomena with perfect catholicity of vision. Such figures and indeed all sculptural embroidery of Indian temples are confined to the exterior walls of the shrine, which is absolutely plain within. Such is the veil of nature's empirical life, enshrining one, not contradicted or identified into variety. (6)

Siva and Parvati, Rajput (Pahari), early 19th century

SCHOOLS OF STYLES OF INDIAN ART

The schools of styles of Indian Art as known by actual remains may be classified as follows:

Early Buddhist, B.C. 300-50 A.D.: pillar edicts, Sanchi and Mahabodhi *stupa*s and railings (all Asokan, 3rd century B.C.); Mathura fragments; Amaravati and Bharhut *stupa*, and Sanchi Gates (2nd century B.C.); Kushan or Greco-Buddhist, 50-320 A.D.; Gandhara sculptures of the Afghanistan frontier; sculpture at Mathura; architecture at Gandhara, and later in Kashmir (Marthand, 8th century); Mahabodhi great temple (ca. 140 A.D.); Besnagar *garuda* pillar; transition of early Buddhist to Gupta at Amaravati (railing, 150-200 A.D.); early painting at Ajanta and in Orissa.

Gupta, 320-600 A.D.: sculpture and architecture (*stupa*, etc.) at Sarnath; at Anuradhapura (2nd century B.C. to 9th century A.D.); sculpture and painting at Ajanta; painting and secular architecture at Sigiriya (Ceylon, 5th century A.D.).

Classic Indian, 600-850 A.D. but especially the 8th century; latest and best painting at Ajanta; sculpture and architecture at Ellora, Elephanta, Mamallapuram, Anuradhapura, and Borubudur (Java).

Medieval, 9th to 18th century (surviving in Ceylon, Travancore, Rajputana, etc., up to the British period, and in Nepal to the present day); Shaivite Bronzes (Nataraja, etc.), sculpture and architecture of Tanjore (10th to 12th century); Vijayanagar (14th to 16th century), Madura (17th century), Auvadaiyar Kovil, Tarapatri (16th century), sculpture and architecture; Chalukyam architecture of Mysore, etc. (Belur, Halebad, 12th to 13th century); sculpture and architecture in Java up to 14th century, in Cambodia to the 12th; Polonnaruva sculpture and architecture (8th to 13th century), Orissa (Bhuvaneswar, Konarak, Puri, 9th to 13th century), Khajuraho (ca. 1000 A.D.); Rajput painting and architecture (up to 19th century); Mughal painting and architecture (16th to 18th century); Nepalese Buddhist bronzes; art of Burma and Siam.

British, 1760-; decline of crafts; survival of architecture; school of art-painting; *swadeshi*; modern Bengali painting. (6)

Seated Buddha from Takht Bahi, Pakistan,
1st century

Standing *Bodhisattva*, Gandhara,
2nd-3rd century

Mahabodhi Temple, Bodh Gaya

View of the Great Stupa, casing slab from
Amaravati *stupa*, 2nd century

Left: Relief from Bharhut; *Center*: Buddha from Mathura; *Right*: Relief from Bharhut

Left: North gate of the Great Stupa of Sanchi, 2nd century; *Right*: A dryad, Great Stupa of Sanchi

Left: Head of the Buddha, Sarnath, 5th century; *Right*: Copper Buddha from Sultanganj, Bihar, 6th century

Left: Naga Dvarapala, Vatadage, Polonnaruva, Ceylon; *Right*: Visnu rescues Gajendra, Deogarh, Uttar Pradesh, early 6th century

A scene from the *Mahajanaka Jataka*, mural in Cave 1, Ajanta

An *apsara*, mural in Cave 17, Ajanta, end of 5th century

Fresco painting of a queen, Sigiriya, Ceylon

Trimurti, Ellora Caves, Maharashtra

Durga slays Mahisasura, Mahabalipuram, 7th century

Kailasanatha Temple, Ellora, 8th century

Bhima and Dharmaraja temples, Mahabalipuram

Trimurti, Elephanta Caves

Left: Standing Buddha, late Anuradhapura period, Ceylon, 800-850; *Right*: Teaching Buddha, Borobudur, Java

Dancer, stone carving from Borobudur

Saint reading, Polonnaruva

Bodhisattva, Cambodia

Scene from the *Ramayana*, Siva Temple, Loro Jonggrang, Eastern Java

Siva, Hoysalesvara Temple, Halebid, 12th century

Celestial with mirror, Chennakesava Temple, Belur, 12th century

Divine attendants, Rajputana, 12th-13th century

Surya, from Konarak Temple

Lingaraja Temple, Bhuvanesvar, Orissa, 11th-12th century

Kandarya Mahadeva Temple, Khajuraho, Madhya Pradesh, c. 1000

Brihadeshwara Temple, Tanjore, Tamil Nadu, 11th century

Arunachaleshwara Temple, Tiruvannamalai, Tamil Nadu, 9th century

Left: Manikka Vacagar, Polonnaruva, 11th-13th century; *Center*: Sundara Murti Swami, Polonnaruva, 11th-13th century; *Right*: Hanuman, Tamil Nadu, 11th century

Left: Siva Vinadhara, Tamil Nadu, 11th century; *Center*: Krishnaraya of Vijayanagar and Queens, Tirupati, early 16th century; *Right*: Parvati, Chola period, 10th century

Siva Nataraja, Southern India, 17th century

Left: Shaiva devotee, Tamil Nadu, 11th century; *Right*: Uma, South India, 12th century

BOROBUDUR

The rich and gracious forms of these reliefs, which if placed end to end would extend for over five kilometers, bespeak an infinitely luxurious rather than a profoundly spiritual or energized experience. There is here no nervous tension, no concentration of force to be compared with that which so impresses the observer at Angkor Wat. Borobudur is like a ripe fruit matured in breathless air; the fullness of its forms is an expression of static wealth, rather than the volume that denotes the outward radiation of power. The Sumatran empire was now in the very height of its glory, and in intimate contact with the whole of the then civilized world; in the last analysis Borobudur is a monument of Sailendra culture, rather than that of Buddhist devotion. (2)

View of Borobudur

SCULPTURE

The best sculpture is primitive rather than suave.... It is like the outward poverty of God, whereby His glory is nakedly revealed. (3)

The purpose of the imager was neither self-expression nor the realization of beauty. He did not choose his own problems, but, like the Gothic sculptor, obeyed a hieratic canon. He did not regard his own or his own fellow's work from the standpoint of connoisseurship of aestheticism—not, that is to say, from the standpoint of the philosopher, or aesthete, but from that of a pious artisan. To him the theme was all in all. (3)

To appreciate any art, we ought not to concentrate our attention upon its peculiarities—ethical or formal—but should endeavor to *take for granted* whatever the artist has taken for granted. No motif appears bizarre to those who have been familiar with it for generations.... (3)

Gupta sculpture, though less ponderous than the ancient types, is still distinguished by its volume; its energy proceeds from within the form, and is static rather than kinetic, a condition that is reversed only in the medieval period. In all these respects Gupta art marks the zenith in a perfectly normal cycle of artistic evolution. (2)

The Hindus do not regard the religious, aesthetic, and scientific standpoints as necessarily conflicting, and in all their finest work, whether musical, literary, or plastic, those points of view, nowadays so sharply distinguished, are inseparably united. (6)

There is a close connection between sculpture and dancing; not merely in as much as certain images represent dancing gods, but because the Indian art of dancing is primarily one of gesture, in which the hands play a most important part. (6)

If any power in Indian art is really unique, it is its marvelous representation of movement—for here in the movement of the limbs is given the swiftness and necessity of the impelling thought itself, much more than a history of action subsequent to thought. (6)

Vitarka mudra

Dhyana mudra

Dharmachakra mudra

Vara mudra

Bhumisparsa mudra

Abhaya mudra

THE BUDDHA IMAGE

Chief Types of Buddha Image: The seated figure has three main forms, the first representing pure *samadhi*, the highest station of ecstasy—here the hands are crossed in the lap in what is known as DHYANA MUDRA, the "seal of meditation" (of Buddha at Anuradhapura); the second, in which the right hand is moved forward across the right knee to touch the earth, in what is known as BHUMISPARSA MUDRA (cf. Painting at Dambulla, Ceylon) the "seal of calling the earth to witness"; ... the third with the hands raised before the chest in the position known as DHARMACHAKRA MUDRA, the "seal of turning the wheel of the law" (cf. Buddha at Sarnath). In a fourth type the right hand is raised and the palm is turned outward, making the gesture known as ABHAYA MUDRA, the "seal of dispelling fear" (cf. Buddhas at Mathura and Anuradhapura). The last pose is characteristic of standing figures, where the left hand grasps the end of the robe. In *bodhisattva* figures the right hand is very often extended in the VARA MUDRA or the "seal of charity" (cf. Avalokitesvara of Nepal), while the left hand holds an attribute, such as the lotus (cf. Gautama Buddha of Ceylon and Avalokitesvara of Nepal). But the variety of *bodhisattvas* is great. Another characteristic pose is known as VITARKA MUDRA, the "seal of argument" indicating the act of teaching (cf. Avalokitesvara Bodhisattva of Ceylon Bronze). Other forms are generally self-explanatory, like the sword of wisdom which is held aloft by Manjusri (cf. Manjusri *bodhisattva* of Java) to cleave the darkness of ignorance. (31)

Manjusri *bodhisattva*, Java

Khusrau Shah swearing fealty to Babur, miniature from *Baburnama*, late 16th century

Abul Fazl ibn Mubarak presenting *Akbarnama* to the Grand Mughal Akbar, Mughal miniature, 16th century

MUGHAL PAINTING

The most characteristic features of Mughal painting are its profound interest in individual character, its analytic rather than synthetic method, and its concern with the doings of kings and courtiers, rather than with the visions of saints or the lyric symbolism of an agricultural race. (*)

The best Mughal work of the 16th century is the most Persian, and of the 17th century the most Indian. The Mughal style of painting (as well as architecture) though built up with the materials of many different traditions is the most undeniably original, in the same sense that the Mughal culture in India is as a whole original. It is true that it combines something new ... it finds its truest expression in the character of such a man as Akbar. (*)

Thus Mughal painting, like the contemporary Memoirs of the Great Mughals, reflects an interest that is exclusively in persons and events; is essentially an art of portraiture and chronicle. (2)

The Rajput painting is deeply religious; the Mughal art is secular, concerned with the doings of princes and courtiers, its outlook upon the present moment. It is not an idealization of life, but a very refined and accomplished representation of a magnificent phase of it. (78)

A Mughal prince visiting the Hindu ascetic Swami Haridas, Rajastan, 18th century

RAJPUT PAINTING

Very different in character is Rajput painting, that Hindu art which as Abul Fazl himself said "surpasses our conception of things." It has a range of content and a depth of passion foreign to the sentimental Persian idylls and battle and hunting scenes, and rarely touched in the Mughal studies of individual character. All the self-restraint and the abandonment, the purity and wild extravagance, the tenderness and the fury of Hinduism find expression here. The art is religious, lyrical, and epic. It has many of the qualities of folk-song and ballad. Portraiture is comparatively rare.... For the Mughal courtier, life was a glorious pageant: for the Rajput and the *brahman*, life was an eternal sacrament. It is a descendent of that art of tempera painting which we lose sight of at Ajanta. (*)

The arms of the lovers are about each other's necks, eye meets eye, the whispering *sakhi*s [confidantes] speak of nothing else but the course of Krishna's courtship, the very animals are spellbound by the sound of his flute, and the elements stand still to hear the ragas and raginis. This art is only concerned with the realities of life; above all, with passionate love service, conceived as the symbol of all union. If Rajput art at first sight appears to lack the material charm of Persian pastorals, or the historic significance of Mughal portraiture, it more than compensates in tenderness and depth of feeling, in gravity and reverence. Rajput art creates a magic world where all men are heroic, all women are beautiful, passionate, and shy, beasts both wild and tame are the friends of man, and trees and flowers are conscious of the footsteps of the bridegroom as he passes by. This magic world is not unreal or fanciful, but a world of imagination and eternity, visible to all who do not refuse to see with the transfiguring eyes of love. (78)

[The Rajput art] is folk art descended from a more magnificent tradition; those who possess the faculty of imaginative reconstruction will catch in this folk art the accents of a loftier speech than that of its intrinsic achievement. (*)

Krishna welcoming Sudama, Jammu, 16th century

Left: Madhu Madhavi Ragini, Rajastan, early 17th century; *Right*: *Hour of Cowdust*, Kangra, late 18th century

Krishna quelling a *naga*, Rajput, Pahari, Kangra, 18th century

Left: *Krishna and Radha*, Pahari, c. 1770
Right: *Siva and Parvati*, Kangra, 18th century

Left: *The Swing*, Kangra, 18th century
Right: *Ragini Tori*, Rajput, 18th century

Krishna and the Gopis, Rajput, Kangra, 18th century

The Royal Exiles [*Sita, Rama, and Lakshmana*] *in a Sage's Hermitage*, Rajput, Pahari, 18th century

JAINA ART

The Jaina art of painting is one of pure draughtsmanship; the pictures are brilliant statements of the facts of the epic, where every event is seen in the light of eternity.... There is no preoccupation with pattern, color, or texture for their own sake, but these are achieved with inevitable assurance in a way that could not have been the case had they been directly sought. The drawing has in fact the perfect equilibrium of a mathematical equation, or a page of composer's score. Theme and formula compose an inseparable unity, text and pictures form a continuous relation of the same dogma in the same key. (48)

Illumination from a Jain manuscript, Gujarat

PERSIAN PAINTING

Persian painting is pretty, even beautiful, it is graceful, lyrical, exquisite in coloring and design, but it is never passionate. It tells us of magnificent adventures and of scented gardens, not of the love of God or the infinite joy and sorrow of the loves of women and men. It does not reveal to us the character of men or the souls of animals and trees and mountains. Its types are conventional rather than ideal, and one wearies of the languid mannerism, notwithstanding its marvelous charm. (*)

Persian miniature, Tabriz, 16th century

Aripana dedicated to Lord Visnu,
folk art from Mithila

Four fishes, symbolizing the power of Lord Visnu over the four headquarters of space,
folk art from Mithila

FOLKLORE

To suppose that old folklore motifs (of which the origin is left unexplained) are taken up into scriptural contexts, in which they survive as foreign bodies, is to invert the order of nature; the fact is that scriptural formulae survive in folklore, it may even be long after the "Scripture" itself has been romanticized or rationalized in more sophisticated circles. In whichever context they are preserved correctly, the motifs retain their intelligibility, whether or not they are actually understood by any given audience. These motifs are not primarily "figures of speech" but "figures of thought," and whoever still understands them is not reading meanings *into* them but only reading *in* them, the significance that was originally concreated with them. (24)

Folk arts preserve symbolic material that is very ancient and of deep significance—even though this may have been partly forgotten nowadays. The folk art is not really *primitive* or naive in the anthropological sense, but preserves the *primordial* symbolism of the metaphysical tradition—mixed, of course, in some cases with more modern elements. (70)

It is only when we realize that the arts and philosophies of our remote ancestors were "fully developed," and that we are dealing with the relics of an ancient *wisdom*, as valid now as it ever was, that the thought of the earliest thinkers will become intelligible to *us*. We shall only be able to understand the astounding uniformity of the folklore motifs all over the world, and the devoted care that has everywhere been taken to ensure their correct transmission, if we approach these *mysteries* (for they are nothing less) in the spirit in which they have been transmitted "from the Stone Age until now"—with the confidence of little children, indeed, but not the childish self-confidence of those who hold that wisdom was born with themselves. The true folklorist must be, not so much a psychologist as a theologian and a metaphysician, if he is to "understand his material." (79)

MUSIC

Music has been a cultivated art in India for at least three thousand years. The chant is an essential element of Vedic ritual; and the references in later Vedic literature, the scriptures of Buddhism, and the Brahmanical epics show that it was already highly developed as a secular art in centuries preceding the beginning of the Christian era. Its zenith may perhaps be assigned to the Imperial age of the Guptas—from the fourth to the sixth century A.D. This was the classic period of Sanskrit literature, culminating in the drama of Kalidasa; and to the same time is assigned the monumental treatise on the theory of music and drama. (3)

Since Indian music is not written, and cannot be learnt from books, except in theory, it will be understood that the only way for a foreigner to learn it must be to establish between himself and his Indian *teachers* that special relationship of disciple and master which belongs to Indian education in all its phases: he must enter into the inner spirit and must adopt many of the outer conventions of Indian life, and his study must continue until he can improvise the songs under Indian conditions and to the satisfaction of Indian professional listeners. He must possess not only the imagination of an artist, but also a vivid memory and an ear sensitive to microtonal inflections. (3)

India has, besides the *tambura,* many solo instruments. By far the most important of these is the *vina.* This classic instrument, which ranks with the violin of Europe and the koto of Japan, and second only to the voice in sensitive response, differs chiefly from the *tambura* in having frets, the notes being made with the left hand and the strings plucked with the right. The delicate nuances of microtonal grace are obtained by deflection of the strings, whole passages being played in this manner solely be a lateral movement of the left hand, without a fresh plucking. While the only difficulty in playing the *tambura* is to maintain an even rhythm independently of the song, the *vina* presents all the difficulties of technique that can be imagined, and it is said that at least twelve years are required to attain proficiency. (3)

The *vina* is the classic solo instrument of Hindu culture, carried always by Sarasvati, goddess of learning and science, and by the *rishi* Narada and by various *raginis.* (7)

This Indian music is essentially impersonal; it reflects an emotion and an experience which are deeper and wider and older than the emotion or wisdom of any single individual. Its sorrow is without tears, its joy without exultation, and it is passionate without any loss of serenity. It is in the deepest sense of the words all-human. But when the Indian prophet speaks of inspiration, it is to say that the *Veda*s are eternal, and all that the poet achieves by his devotion is to hear, to see: it is then Sarasvati, the goddess of speech and learning, or Narada, whose mission it is to disseminate occult knowledge in the sound of the strings of his *vina*, or Krishna, whose flute is forever calling us to leave the duties of the world and follow Him—it is these, rather than any human individual, who speak through the singer's voice, and are seen in the movements of the dancer. (3)

The Indian singer is a poet, and the poet a singer. The dominant subject matter of the songs is human or divine love in all its aspects, or the direct praise of God, and the words are always sincere and passionate. The more essentially the singer is a musician, however, the more the words are regarded merely as the vehicle of the music: in art-song the words are always brief, voicing a mood rather than telling any story, and they are used to support the music with little regard to their own logic—precisely as the representative element in a modern painting merely serves as the basis for an organization of pure form or color. (3)

A *vina* player

A *sarod* player

AN INDIAN MUSICAL PARTY

Perhaps you are in the south. You have gone to a musical party, a wedding at the house of a friend, you are seated with many others on the cotton carpet, and before you is a band of drummers, oboists, and players of the *vina* and *tambura*. A *brahman* drums on an earthen pot. A slender girl of fifteen years sits demurely on the floor, dressed in silk brocade and golden chains, her feet and arms bare, and flowers in her hair. Her mother is seated near, back against the wall; she it is that trained the girl, and now she watches her proudly. The only sounds are those of the four strings of the ivory inlaid *tambura* and the tapping of the drum. As you are waiting for the music to begin, a man with untidy hair and a saffron robe comes in, and your host gives him eager welcome, laying a white cloth on a stool for him to sit upon. All know him well—he is a *sannyasin* who wanders from temple to temple, preaching little, nor performing many ceremonies, but singing *tevarams* and the hymns of Manikka Vacagar. As he sits silent, all eyes are turned towards him, and conversation drops to a whisper. Presently he sings some hymn of passionate adoration of Siva. His voice is thin but very sweet, melting the heart; his gentle strong personality holds every listener spellbound not least the little dancer to whom the words and music are so familiar; he is the dancer's and the drummers' friend and hero as much as yours. Someone asks for a special hymn, "My God, why hast thou forsaken me?" and he sings:

Me, meanest one, in mercy mingling Thou didst make Thine own,
Lord of the Bull! Lo, thou'st forsaken me! O Thou who wear'st
Garb of fierce tiger's skin! Abiding Uttarakosamangai's King!
Thou of the braided lock! I fainting sink. Our Lord, uphold thou me!
What though I press no more the crimson lips of maidens fair,
With swelling breasts; behold! Thou hast forsaken me; though in,
Not out Thy worthy service, Uttarakosamangai's King,
I am! Thou mad'st false me Thine own, why dost Thou leave me now?[1]

Soon he rises, smiles at the musicians and speaks for a few moments with your host, and so goes away. And then you forget for a time this dreamer, in the beauty of the dance and the clamor of the drums. Of the dance you

[1] Adapted from the translation by Dr. Pope.

never weary; there is eternal wonder in the perfect refinement of its grace, and the mental concentration needed to control each muscle so completely; for this is not the passionate posturing born of a passing mood, but the elaborated art of three thousand years, an art that deceives you by its seeming simplicity, but in reality idealizes every passion, human and divine; for it tells of the intensity of Radha's love for Krishna. Radha was the leader of the herd-girls in Brindaban, and she, more than any, realized the depth and sweetness of the love of Krishna.

Krishna playing the flute for the *gopis*, Kangra miniature, 18th century

Whatever place is held in the heart of Europe by the love of Dante for his Lady Beatrice, of Paolo for Francesca, of Deirdre for Naoisi, is held in India by the love stories of Rama and Sita, of Padmavati and Ratan Sen, and the love of Radha and Krishna. Most wonderful of these was the love of Radha; in the absolute self-surrender of the human soul in her to the Divine in Krishna is summed up all love. In this consecration of humanity there is no place for the distinction—always foreign to Indian thought—of sacred and profane. But when in love the finite is brought into the presence of the infinite, when the consciousness of inner and outer is destroyed in the ecstasy of union with one beloved, the moment of realization is expressed in Indian poetry, under the symbol of the speech of Radha, the leader of the *gopis*,

The Musical Mode Gauri, from a Ragamala series, Pahari, c. 1770

with Krishna the Divine Cowherd. And Krishna is the Lord, Radha, the soul that strives in self-surrender, for inseparable oneness. And so both have told of the Lord—the ascetic, for whom all earthly beauty is a vain thing, and the dancing girl, who is mistress of every art that charms the senses.

The music is to last all night; but you have to be home ere dawn, and as you pass along the road in the bright moonlight, you see that life, and the renunciation of life, lead both to the same goal at last. Both ascetic and musician shall be one *Brahman* with himself; it is only a question of time more or less, and time, as everyone knows, is unreal.

Oh Lord, look not upon my evil qualities!
Thy name, O Lord, is same-sightedness,
Make us both one Brahman.

This Hindu song of Surdas is said to have been sung by a dancing girl at a Rajput court. And there comes to you to the thought, that "Whoso seeth all beings in That One, and That in all, henceforth shall doubt no more."

All this is passing away; when it is gone, men will look back on it with hungry eyes, as some have looked upon the life even of Medieval Europe, or of Greece. When civilization has made of life a business, it will be remembered that life was once an art; when culture is the privilege of bookworms, it will be remembered that it was once a part of life itself, not something achieved in stolen moments of relief from the serious business of being an engine-driver, a clerk, or a Governor.

Let those who are still part of such a life take note of it, that they may tell their children of it when it is nothing but a memory. A "practical" and "respectable" world has no place for the dreamer and the dancer; they belong to the old Hindu towns where the big temples and the chatrams tell of the faith and munificence of kings and merchant princes. In Madras, there is the military band, or the music hall company on tour—what does it want with ascetics or with dancing girls? (5)

A Celebration for Shah Jahan, Mughal miniature, c. 1635

JEWELRY

From the earliest times the Indians have loved to adorn themselves with jewels, indeed, the modern work descends in an unbroken line from the primitive and still surviving use of garlands of fresh flowers, and of seeds. From these are derived the names of the work in gold, such as champabud necklace. Many of the names of jewels mentioned in Panini's grammar (4th century B.C.) are still in use. The long Punjabi necklaces are called "garlands of enchantment," *mohanmala*, earrings are called ear flowers (*karn phul*). The forms are suggestive but never imitative of the flower prototypes. Perhaps no people in the world have loved jewelry so well as the Indians. It is a religious duty to provide a wife with jewels as with dress; she should never appear before her husband without them, but in his absence on a journey she should discard them temporarily, and after his death forever. One need be an Indian woman, born and bred in the great tradition to realize the sense of power that such jewels as earrings and anklets lend their wearers; she knows the full delight of swinging jewels touching her cheeks at every step, and the fascination of the tinkling bells upon her anklets. Some have called her nose-rings barbarous and her love of jewels childish, but there are also those who think that she knows best what best becomes her. (6)

It was highly characteristic of Indian art that these "garlands" should be in design entirely suggestive and in no way imitative of the forms suggested. No Indian craftsman sets a flower in a vase before him and worries out of it some sort of ornament by taking thought.... For a decorative art not intimately related to his own experience can have no intrinsic vitality. And so the goldsmith's chains are not like real flowers, but they mean flowers to himself and to the wearer of them.

The same principles apply to the treatment of birds in jewelry. To wear a real bird would be considered barbarous and to imitate a real bird very closely would be idle.... But all that is beautiful in the general idea of the bird form and poise can be suggested. (7)

It is a compliment to true Sinhalese art to say that the jewelry now made has nothing characteristically Sinhalese about it. With the loss of the traditions of good design, has gone the capacity for fine work; not only is it impossible to get fine old work copied, but modern settings in particular are so insecure that the stones frequently fall out in a few days. Sinhalese jewelry today had indeed sunk to "the level of the extravagantly hard and vulgar trinketry of Birmingham, Paris, and Vienna." (7)

Top left: Silver waist-chain, Ceylon; *Top right*: *Gauri shankar* gold bead, Ceylon; *Bottom left*: Bird-pendant, Ceylon; *Bottom center*: Setting of a knife, Ceylon; *Bottom right*: Nut slicer, Ceylon

3. RELIGION

The Temple at Chidambaram dedicated to Lord Siva, Tamil Nadu

RELIGION

Our modern antipathy to religion, and our social reluctance to speak of God, are largely the result of the "sentimentalizing" of religion, and the general endeavor to make of the great religious heroes, notably the Christ and the Buddha, the sort of men we can approve of and also by an elimination of the marvelous features in their "lives," the sort of men to whom we can attribute an historical reality, and in whom we can therefore "believe"; we are bewildered by the man who can say "I know that my Redeemer liveth," but is far from being convinced that he ever lived. (15)

The multiplicity of the forms of images, coinciding with the development of monotheistic Hinduism, arises from various causes, all ultimately referable to the diversity of need of individuals and groups. In particular, this multiplicity is due historically to the inclusion of all pre-existing forms, all local forms, in a greater theological synthesis, where they are interpreted as modes of emanation of the supreme *Isvara.* (30)

One must have learned that an access to reality cannot be had by making a choice between matter and spirit considered as things unlike in all respects, but rather by seeing in things material and sensible a formal likeness to spiritual prototypes of which the senses can give no direct report. (82)

There are many gods in the Hindu pantheon, but they are no more than the imaginative shadowing forth of an all-compassing, all penetrating spirit. (*)

Hinduism emerges, not as a post-Vedic development, a theistic declension from the lofty visions of the *Upanisad*s, but as something handed on from a prehistoric past, ever-changing and yet ever essentially itself, raised at various times by devotional ecstasy and philosophic speculation to heights beyond the grasp of thought, and yet preserving in its popular aspects the most archaic rites and animistic imagery. (42)

There always remains a last step, in which the ritual is abandoned and the relative truths of theology are denied. As it was by the knowledge of good and evil that man fell from his first estate, so it must be from the knowledge of good and evil, from the moral law, that he must be delivered at last. However far one may have gone, there remains a last step to be taken, involving a dissolution of all former values. A church or society—the Hindu would make no distinction—that does not provide a way of escape from its own regimen, and will not let its people go, is defeating its own ultimate purpose. (28)

It is of the essence of a mystery, and above all of the *Mysterium Magnum*, that it cannot be communicated, but only realized: all that can be communicated are its external supports or symbolic expressions; the Great Work must be done by everyone for himself.... The Way has been charted in detail by every Forerunner, who *is* the Way; what lies at the end of the road is not revealed, even by those who have reached it, because it cannot be told and does not appear: the Principle is not in any likeness. (24)

Dharma is that morality by which a given social order is protected. "It is by *Dharma* that civilization is maintained" (*Matsya Purana*, cxlv. 27). *Dharma* may also be translated as social norm, moral law, vocation, function, order, duty, righteousness, or as religion, mainly in its exoteric aspects. (52)

For there are many of these Hindus and Buddhists whose knowledge of Christianity and of the greatest Christian writers is virtually nil, as there are Christians, equally learned whose real knowledge of any other religion but their own is virtually nil, because they have never imagined what it might be to live these other faiths. Just as there can be no real knowledge of a language if we have never even imaginatively participated in the activities to which the language refers so there can be no real knowledge of any "life" that one has not in some measure lived. (40)

The last end of every human activity is the knowledge of God, and it is our duty to refer all our acts to our last end. (*)

Let us not forget even for a moment that there exists an ultimate universal power which is always within man, and which makes itself known in the world through man. (*)

THE *BHAGAVAD GITA*

We must, however, especially mention the *Bhagavad Gita* as probably the most important single work ever produced in India; this book of eighteen chapters is not, as it has been sometimes called, a "sectarian" work, but one universally studied and often repeated daily from memory by millions of Indians of all persuasions; it may be described as a compendium of the whole Vedic doctrine to be found in the earlier *Veda*s, *Brahmana*s and *Upanisad*s, and being therefore the basis of all the latest developments, it can be regarded as the focus of all Indian religion. To this we must add that the pseudo-historical Krishna and Arjuna are to be identified with the mythical Agni and Indra. (28)

A very large number of Hindus, very many millions certainly, daily repeat from memory a part, or in some cases even the whole, of the *Bhagavad Gita*. This recitation is a chanting; and no one who has heard Sanskrit poetry thus recited, as well as understanding it, can really judge of it as poetry. The style is quite simple and without ornament, like that of the rest of the Epic, and the *Upanisads*; it is not yet the ornamented classical style of the Dramas. On the whole I think the judgments of professional scholars are to be dis-

Krishna reveals the *Bhagavad Gita* to Arjuna

counted; for many reasons personally, I should think a good comparison, poetically, would be with the best of medieval Latin hymns. (32)

The universal acceptance of the *Bhagavad Gita*, in which the *Upanishad* doctrines, combined with the path of devotion to a personal deity and of spiritual progress through selfless fulfillment of vocation are first and fully set forth. (39)

The orthodox conception of devotional religion thus evolved is summarized with supreme genius in the most popular of all Indian scriptures, the *Bhagavad Gita*—the one book with which the student of India, even the student of Indian art if he confines himself to a single book, should familiarize himself. Here we find the religious philosophy of Indian society, not that of any particular ascetic order. The teaching is that spiritual freedom (*moksa*, *nirvana*, the *summun bonum*, here conceived in terms of union with the Supreme Being) is best attained through a selfless devotion to the fulfillment of function (*dharma*), and by loving devotion to the deity, under whatsoever form he may be worshipped. (44)

The *Bhagavad Gita* is also the chief gospel of action without attachment: change, says Krishna, is the law of life, therefore act according to duty, not clinging to any object of desire, but like the actor in a play, who knows that his mask (*persona*-lity) is not himself. (7)

The *Bhagavad Gita* (in the *Mahabharata*) consists of a dialogue between Krishna and the hero Arjuna, on the eve of battle. Arjuna puts forward pacifistic objections to the slaying of kinsmen in battle for the sake of empire. Krishna in reply expounds the doctrine of *svadharma* ("own duty"), i.e. the performance of the function appropriate to one's born status (caste); the path of action (*karma-marga*) is incumbent on the individual, and the surest means of spiritual progress: "therefore fight." The philosophy of the *Upanisads* affords consolation: it is only these mortal bodies of men in which That One (*Brahman*, *Purusa*) manifests continually, that can be slain: Arjuna should not be dismayed by what we now call the problem of evil, since That One, the only reality, cannot be injured or slain. Arjuna is still bewildered by the liability of man to error. Krishna replies to this by expounding the doctrine of *bhakti*, loving devotion to the deity (himself): "One who renounces the fruit of actions (is without personal ambition), and worships Me with undivided heart, be it even a sinner, a woman, or a *sudra*, I release from the cycle of transmigration, he comes unfailingly to Me." And who is Krishna? "No one knoweth Me; beyond this manifested self, hidden therein by the three *gunas* and by *Maya* is my higher, timeless Being. I am the source of the forthgoing of the Universe, and the place of its dissolution; all this is strung on Me, like rows of pearls upon a thread; I have no needs, nor ends to be accomplished; I mingle in action only lest righteousness should fail on earth." He who decides to read only one book on India should read the *Bhagavad Gita*; for though in form it is specifically *Vaisnava*, its application is universal and it is read and known by heart to millions, of all sects. All the guiding forces of Indian civilization, and much of its detail, are to be found in the *Gita*, enunciated in language of unsurpassed power and beauty. (44)

The *Gita* or song, has become a gospel universally acceptable to all Indian sects. No single work of equal length so well expresses the characteristic trend of Indian thought, or so completely depicts the Indian ideal of character. It speaks of diverse ways of salvation—that is, escaping from self and knowing God: by love, by works, and by learning. God has two modes of being, the unmanifest and unconditioned, the manifest and conditioned. (29)

श्रीभगवानुवाच
कालोऽस्मि लोकक्षयकृत् प्रवृद्धो
लोकान् समाहर्तुमिह प्रवृत्तः ।
ऋतेऽपि त्वां न भविष्यन्ति सर्वे
येऽवस्थिताः प्रत्यनीकेषु योधाः ॥ ३२ ॥

Bhagavad Gita, 11:32

THE SELF

It is incorrect to call the soul "immortal" indiscriminately, just as it is incorrect to call any man a genius. Man has an immortal SOUL, as he has a GENIUS, but the soul can only be immortalized by returning to its source, that is to say, by dying to itself and living to its Self, just as man becomes a genius only when he is no longer himself. (89)

Impassivity is not less characteristic of the faces of the gods in moments of ecstatic passion or destroying fury, than the face of the stillest Buddha. In each, emotion is interior, and the features show no trace of it: only the movements or the stillness of the limbs express the immediate purpose of the actor. That it is "this body," not the inmost Self that acts, "that slayeth or is slain" is as clearly expressed in the Vedic literature. (6)

He only is free from virtues and vices and all their fatal consequences who never became anyone; he only can be free who is no longer anyone; impossible to be freed from oneself and also to remain oneself. The liberation from good and evil that seemed impossible and is impossible for the man whom we define by what he does or thinks and who answers the question "Who is that?", "It's me," is possible only for him who can answer at the Sundoor to the question "Who art thou?", "Thyself." (28)

Such an one no longer loves himself or others, but is the Self in himself and in them. Death to one's self is death to "others"; and if the "dead man" seems to be "unselfish," this will not be the result of altruistic motives, but accidentally, and because he is literally un-self-ish. Liberated from himself, from all status, all duties, all rights, he has become a Mover-at-will (*kamachari*), like the Spirit (*Vayu, atma devanam*) that "moveth as it will" (*yatha vasham charati*), and as Saint Paul expresses it, "no longer under the law." (28)

Individuality is motivated by and perpetuated by wanting; and the cause of all wanting is "ignorance" (*avidya*)—for we "ignore" that the objects of our desire can never be possessed in any real sense of the word, ignore that even when we have got what we want, we still "want" to keep it and are still "in want." The ignorance meant is of things as they really are, and the consequent attribution of substantiality to what is merely phenomenal; the seeing of Self in what is not-Self. (28)

OM

Of all the names and forms of God the monogrammatic syllable *Om*, the totality of all sounds and the music of the spheres chanted by the resonant Sun, is the best. (28)

The sacred syllable *Om*

An Ascetic, Rajput, 17th century

YOGA

This is the practice of *yoga*, whereby enlightenment and emancipation are sought to be attained by meditation calculated to release the individual from empirical consciousness....

The essence of the method lies in the concentration of thought upon a single point, carried so far that the duality of subject and object is resolved into a perfect unity—"when," in the words of Schelling, "the perceiving self merges in the self-perceived. At that moment we annihilate time and the duration of time; we are no longer in time, but time, or rather eternity itself, is in us." A very beautiful description of the *yogi* is given as follows in the *Bhagavad Gita*, and as quoted here in a condensed form applies almost equally to Buddhist and Brahmanical practice, for the *yoga* is a praxis rather than a form of sectarian belief:

> *Abiding alone in a secret place, without craving and without possessions, he shall take his seat upon a firm seat, neither over-high nor over-low, and with the working of the mind and of the senses held in check, with body, head, and neck maintained in perfect equipoise, looking not round about him, so let him meditate, and thereby reach the peace of the Abyss; and the likeness of one such, who knows the boundless joy that lies beyond the senses and is grasped by intuition, and who swerves not from truth, is that of a lamp in a windless place that does not flicker.* (3)

HINDUISM & BUDDHISM

The more superficially one studies Buddhism, the more it seems to differ from the Brahmanism in which it originated; the more profound our study, the more difficult it becomes to distinguish Buddhism from Brahmanism, or to say in what respects, if any, Buddhism is really unorthodox. (28)

Hinduism and Buddhism. The two schools (Hinayanistic and Mahayanistic) originally flourished together in Burma, Siam, Cambodia, Java, and Bali, side by side with a Hinduism with which they often combined. (28)

It would hardly be an exaggeration to say that a faithful account of Hinduism might well be given in the form of a categorical denial of most of the statements that have been made about it, alike by European scholars and by Indians trained in our modern skeptical and evolutionary modes of thought. (38)

Buddha Sakyamuni, Lopburi style, 13th-14th century

BIRTH, DEATH, & REINCARNATION

There is no death of anyone save in appearance only, even as there is no birth of anyone, but in appearance only. For when anything turns away from its Essence to assume a nature there is the notion of "birth," and in the same way when it turns away from the nature, to the Essence, there is the notion of a "death," but in truth there is neither a coming into being nor a destruction of any essence, but it is only manifest at one time and invisible at another.

This manifestation and invisibility are due respectively to the density of the material assumed on the one hand, and to the tenuity of the essence on the other.[1] (61)

Reincarnation is not an orthodox Indian doctrine, but only a popular belief. (28)

Life is a flame, and transmigration, new becoming, rebirth, is the transmitting of the flame from one combustible aggregate to another; just that, and nothing more. If we light one candle from another, the communicated flame is one and the same, in the sense of observed continuity, but the candle not the same. (31)

[1] Coomaraswamy's translation of Apollonius' *Epistle to Valerius* (Ep. 58)

VEDANTA & PHILOSOPHY

All that India or any people can offer to the world proceeds from her philosophy. Of course, every race must solve its own problems, and those of its own day. I do not suggest that the ancient Indian solution of the special Indian problems, though its lessons may be many and valuable, can be directly applied to modern conditions. The Brahmanical idea is an Indian "City of the gods"—as *devanagari*, the name of the Sanskrit script, suggests. The building of that city anew the constant task of civilization; and though the details of our plan may change, and the contour of our building, we may learn from India to build on the foundations of the religion of Eternity.

Where the Indian mind differs most from the average mind of Modern Europe is in its views of the value of philosophy. In Europe and America the study of philosophy is regarded as an end in itself, and as such it seems of but little importance to the ordinary man. In India, on the contrary, philosophy is not regarded primarily as a mental gymnastic, but rather with deep religious conviction, as our salvation (*moksa*) from the ignorance (*avidya*) which forever hides from our eyes the vision of reality. Philosophy is the key to the map of life, by which are set forth the meaning of life and the means of attaining its goal. It is no wonder, then, that the Indians have pursued the study of philosophy with enthusiasm, for these are matters which concern all. (3)

The Vedanta is not a "philosophy" in the current sense of the word, but only as the word is used in the phrase *Philosophia Perennis*, and only if we have in mind the Hermetic "philosophy" or that "Wisdom" by whom Boethius was consoled. Modern philosophies are closed systems, employing the method of dialectics, and taking for granted that opposites are mutually exclusive. In modern philosophy things are either so or not so; in eternal philosophy this depends upon our point of view. Metaphysics is not a system, but a consistent doctrine; it is not merely concerned with conditioned and quantitative experience but with universal possibility. (80)

PHILOSOPHIA PERENNIS

The Indian tradition is one of the forms of the *Philosophia Perennis*, and as such, embodies those universal truths to which no one people or age can make exclusive claim. The Hindu is therefore perfectly willing to have his own scriptures made use of by others as "extrinsic and probable proofs" of the truth as *they* also know it. The Hindu would argue, moreover, that it is upon these heights alone that any true agreement of differing cultures can be effected. (28)

During many years I have collected from Eastern and Western sources parallel passages in which identical doctrines have been enunciated as nearly as possible in the same term and often, indeed, in the same idioms and making use of etymologically equivalent words; not at all with a view to the demonstration of any literary "influences," but only to show that the doctrines themselves are cognate in the same sense that the etymons, e.g. of Greek and Sanskrit, are cognate, that is to say, of common origin. (33)

There is only one mythology, one iconography, and one truth, that of an uncreated wisdom that has been handed down from time immemorial. (40)

Many of us are not yet, or are no longer, blinded by an ambition to be in any sense your rivals, to convert you to our ways of thinking, or persuade you to adopt our social patterns; our hope is only that your world may come to its own senses and return to that "inheritance" of truth that must be called the birthright of all mankind, if it be true that, as St. Ambrose says, "All that is true, by whomsoever it has been said, is from the Holy Spirit," whom we all alike acknowledge when we admit a divine paternity, and whom, in the words of St. Augustine, "The whole human race confesses to be the author of the world." (10)

The Christian is invited to participate in a symposium (of religions)—not to preside—for there is Another who presides unseen—but as one of many guests. (25)

Religions may and must be many, each being an "arrangement of God," and stylistically differentiated, inasmuch as the thing known can only be in the knower according to the mode of the knower, and hence as we say in India, "He takes the forms that are imagined by His worshipers," or as Eckhart expresses it, "I am the cause that God is God." And this is why religious beliefs, as much as they have united men, have also divided men against each other, as Christian or heathen, orthodox or heretical. So that if we are to consider what may be the most urgent practical task to be resolved by the philosopher, we can only answer that this is to be recognized in a control and revision of the principles of comparative religion, the true end of which science … should be to demonstrate the common metaphysical basis of all religions and that diverse cultures are fundamentally related to one another as being the dialects of a common spiritual and intellectual language; for whoever realizes this, will no longer wish to assert that "My religion is best," but only that it is the "best for me." (83)

SYMBOLISM

Symbolism and imagery (*pratika*, *pratibimba*, etc), the purest form of art, is the proper language of metaphysics. (69)

Symbolism is a language and a precise form of thought; a hieratic and a metaphysical language and not a language determined by somatic or psychological categories. Its foundation is in analogical correspondence of all orders of reality and states of being or levels of reference.... Symbolism is a calculus in the same sense that an adequate analogy is a proof. (82)

We are not, then, "reading meaning into" primitive works of art when we discuss their formal principles and final causes, treating them as symbols and supports of contemplation rather than as objects of a purely material utility, but simply *reading their meaning*. (84)

A Nepalese *mandala*

A thing is not only what it is visibly, but also what it represents. Natural or artificial objects are not ... arbitrary "symbols" of some other and higher reality, but actual manifestations of this reality: the eagle or the lion, for example, is not so much a symbol or image *of* the Sun as it *is* the Sun in a likeness (the form being more important than the nature in which it may be manifested); and in the same way every house *is* the world in a likeness, and every altar is situated at the center of the earth; it is only because "we" are more interested in what things are than in what they mean, more interested in particular facts than in universal ideas, that this is "inconceivable" to us. Descent from a totem animal is not, then, what it appears to the anthropologist, a literal absurdity, but a descent from the Sun, the Progenitor and Prajapati of all, in that form in which he revealed himself whether in vision or in dream, to the founder of the clan.... So that, as Lévy-Bruhl says of such symbols, "very often it is not their purpose to 'represent' their prototype to the eye, but to facilitate a participation," and that "if it is their essential function to 'represent,' in the full sense of the word, invisible beings or objects, and to make their presence effective, it follows that they are not necessarily reproductions or likenesses of these beings or objects." (24)

The symbolism of the ferry (Skr. *tirtha*, crossing place) coincides with that of the bridge and the ladder. You know the expression "reaching the farther shore" = liberation. The sea or river of life *flows* between this shore and that shore. One crosses, either by a boat or bridge or ladder: accordingly "as the journey is thought of as a voyage or a climb." So Buddha and Mahavira are *tirthankaras*, "*ferry makers*," a word which corresponds in the other symbolism to our pontifex, pontiff "bridge builder," Pali *setu karatea.* I have collected much material for an article on the "bridge" and some on the "ferry." Amongst Vedic references might be mentioned just X.30.14, a prayer to the Asvins, "make ye a crossing place, or ferry (*krtam tirtham*), i.e. "be *tirthankaras*", and X.53.8, "Stand up and cross over" (*pra tarata*) from the same root *tr* as in *tirtha.* (62)

FAITH

In the discussion of faith it is too often overlooked that the greater part of our knowledge of "things," even of those by which our worldly actions are regulated, is "authoritative"; most, indeed, even of our daily activities would come to an end if we did not believe the words of those who have seen what we have not yet seen, but might see if we would do what they have done, or go where they have been; in the same way those of the Buddhist neophyte would come to an end if he did *not* "believe" in a goal not yet attained. Actually, he believes that the Buddha is telling him the truth, and acts accordingly (*Digha-Nikaya*, II.93). Only the Perfect Man is "faithless," in the sense that in his case knowledge of the Unmade has taken the place of faith (*Dhammapada*, 97), for which there is no more need. (81)

One must believe in order to understand and understand in order to believe. These are not successive, however, but simultaneous acts of the mind. In other words, there can be no knowledge of anything to which the will refuses its consent, or love of anything that has not been known. (80)

SIVA

Siva is represented iconographically, "non-manifest," by the *lingam*, usually established in the main shrine of a temple, and by a great variety of manifested forms, both gracious and terrible. Of all these forms, the best known and perhaps the most significant is that of Nataraja ("Lord of the Dance") presenting the cosmic activity of the deity—more particularly, the Five Activities, or Powers of Creation, Maintenance, Destruction, and the Embodiment and Release of souls: "Our Lord is the Dancer, who like the heat latent in firewood, diffuses his power in mind and matter and makes

Siva Nataraja

them dance in their turn." The worship of this deity in this form is only truly accomplished when the cosmic dance is realized as taking place within the consciousness of the devotee himself, in accordance with the Sanskrit text, *devambhutva, devam yajet*—"only by becoming the god, may he worship the god." It will be seen that the two icons: the "non-manifest" *lingam* and the manifested Nataraja, represent concepts comparable with Ruysbroeck's divine theology in which the nature of God is described as at once Eternal Rest and Eternal Work. (39)

Siva is here represented as Cosmic Dancer. He is four-armed, and has flowery-braided locks ending in tight curls, and whirling in the dance. On the proper right side, in the flying hair, is a figure of Ganga (represented as a *nagini*), on the left a cobra and the crescent moon. The headdress contains a skull and terminates in a fan of Cassia leaves; a pearl fillet encircles the forehead; a man's earring is worn on the proper side, a woman's on the left. Of the four hands the rear right holds a drum (*udukkai*), the rear left a flame in a dish; the front right is in *abhaya mudra* ("do not fear"), the front left hand points to the lifted foot. Amongst the many ornaments are small bells tied round the calf of the leg, as morris-dancers wear them. The whole figure is enclosed in a fiery arch (*tiruvasi*), arising from the mouths of a pair of addorsed makaras, established on a lotus pedestal (*padmasana*).

A legend is told in explanation of this dance (in the *Periya Puranam*), as follows: "In the forest of Taragam there dwelt multitudes of heretical *rishi*s, followers of the Mimamsa. Siva proceeded there to confute them, accompanied by Visnu disguised as a beautiful woman, and by Visnu's servant Ati-Sesan, the *naga* Ananta. The *rishi*s were at first led to dispute amongst themselves, but their anger was soon directed against Siva, and they endeavored to destroy Him by means of incantations. A fierce tiger was produced in the magic fires, and rushed upon Him; but he seized it in his hands, and stripped off its skin with the nail of his little finger, and wrapped it about himself as a garment. The sages renewed their offerings, and produced a monstrous serpent, which Siva took in his hands and wreathed about his neck like a garland. Then He began to dance; but there rushed upon Him a last monster in the shape of a malignant dwarf, Muyalaka. Upon him the God pressed the tip of his foot, and broke the creature's back, so that it writhed upon the ground; then He resumed the dance, beheld of gods and *rishi*s. On this occasion Ati-Sesan obtained the boon to behold the dance again in Tillai, sacred Chitambaram—the center of the Universe (that is, as we shall see below, in one's own heart)."

More significant than the details of this legend, are the interpretations constantly referred to in the Saiva hymns. The dance, called Nadanta, represents the movement of energy within the universe: it is Siva's "Five-Activities," Creation, Preservation, Destruction, Embodiment, and Release. The drum is for Creation (through sound, which, for the Hindus, has always a molding force on the material environment), the flame for Destruction (by fire). The dwarf is Illusion, Plural Perception, the fetters of Time, Space, and Causality, the sense of Egoity, in general, *avidya*.[1] The flaming *tiruvasi* circle represents awakened matter (Nature), vibrant in response to the informing energy which touches its bounds above and below and on either side. The whole conception further implies the well-known myth of the days and nights of Brahma—reconciliation of time and eternity by repeated phase alternations of manifestation and withdrawal.[2] The Sakti of Siva is the Mother of the Universe, as He its Father: She is at once his Energy and Grace. "Let me set upon my head," says St. Arunandi, "the gracious feet of this Our Mother, who cuts the fetters of rebirth and is seated with Our Father in the hearts of the Freed." It is only through and with Sakti, who is part of himself, indeed, that Siva operates in the universe; Siva and Sakti are the sun and its radiance. (47)

This magnificent South Indian bronze, now in the Madras Museum, has often been figured and described. It is probably the finest of the many figures of the "Dancing Lord" to be found in museums (there are examples at Colombo,[3] Copenhagen, the Musée Guimet, South Kensington and elsewhere). The poise and movement make the figure an embodiment of rhythm, and the shapely limbs, especially the lifted leg, are peculiarly beautiful. Siva's dance has both an anecdotal and an esoteric interpretation. The former is as follows: Siva appeared in disguise amongst a congregation of ten thousand sages, and in the course of disputation, confuted them and so angered them thereby, that they endeavored by incantations to destroy Him. A fierce tiger was created in sacrificial flames, and rushed upon Him; but smiling gently, He seized it with His sacred hands, and with the nail of His little finger stripped off its skin, which He wrapped about Himself as if

[1] It should be observed, at the same time, that the trampled figures of Indian sculpture have usually the same attributes as the God, and thus appear to represent rather Time-bound phases (*amsa*) of the God, than anything like a devil. In no case can the dwarf figure be identified with Yama.

[2] For a more detailed discussion see *Siddhanta Dipika*, XIII.1 (July 1912).

[3] See P. Arunachalam, *Spolia Zeylanica*, Vol. VI, Part 22, Sep. 1909, where nearly all are illustrated.

Siva Nataraja, Madras Museum

it had been a silken cloth. Undiscouraged by failure, the sages renewed their offerings, and there was produced a monstrous serpent, which He seized and wreathed about His neck. Then He began to dance; but there rushed upon Him a last monster in the shape of a hideous malignant dwarf. Upon him the God pressed the tip of His foot, and broke the creature's back, so that it writhed upon the ground; and so, His last foe prostrate, Siva resumed the dance of which the gods were witnesses. A modern interpretation of this legend explains that He wraps about Him, as a garment, the tiger fury of human passion; the guile and malice of mankind He wears as a necklace, and beneath His feet is forever crushed the embodiment of evil.... Siva is thus one with that Eros Protogonos, Lord of Life and Death, of whom Lucian spoke when he said, "It would seem that dancing came into being at the beginning of all things, and was brought to light together with Eros, that ancient one for we see this primeval dancing clearly set forth in the choral dance of the constellations, and in the planets and fixed stars, their interweaving and interchange and orderly harmony." Of concrete symbols associated with the dancing figure, the drum in one right hand signifies creative sound, the vibratory movement initiating evolution; the flame in one left hand signifies the converse activity, destruction, involution. The hand upraised (in *abhaya mudra*) says to the worshipper, Fear not; and the other points to His Foot, the refuge of the soul. The Ganges (as a mermaid) and the crescent moon, which should appear in the streaming hair, are not distinguishable in the photograph. A cobra wreathes itself about His arm. Upon His brow blazes the third eye of spiritual wisdom. (47)

It may not be out of place to call attention to the grandeur of this conception (Nataraja) itself as a synthesis of science, religion, and art. How amazing the range of thought and sympathy of those *rishi*-artists who first conceived such a type as this, affording an image of reality, a key to the complex tissue of life, a theory of nature, not merely satisfactory to a single clique or race, nor acceptable to the thinkers of one century only but universal in its appeal to the philosopher, the lover, and the artist of all ages and all countries. How supremely great in power and grace this dancing image must appear to all those who have striven in plastic forms to give expression to their intuition of Life....

Every part of such an image as this is directly expressive, not of any mere superstition or dogma, but of evident facts. No artist of today, however great, could more exactly or more wisely create an image of that Energy which science must postulate behind all phenomena. If we would reconcile Time with Eternity, we can scarcely do so otherwise than by the conception of alterations of phase extending over vast regions of space and great tracts of time. Especially significant, then, is the phase alternation implied by the drum, and the fire which changes, not destroys. These are but visual symbols of the theory of the day and night of Brahma.

In the night of Brahma, Nature is inert, and cannot dance till Siva wills it: He rises from His rapture, and dancing sends through inert matter pulsing waves of awakening sound, lo! matter also dances appearing as a glory round about Him. Dancing, He sustains its manifold phenomena. In the fullness of time, still dancing, he destroys all forms and names by fire and gives new rest. This is poetry; but none the less, science.

It is not strange that the figure of Nataraja has commanded the adoration of so many generations past: familiar with all skepticism, expert in tracing all beliefs to primitive superstitions, explorers of the infinitely great and infinitely small, we are worshippers of Nataraja still. (3)

Siva Nataraja, Polonnaruva, 11th century

Siva can be represented as Gangadhara, "He who bears the river", a title which alludes to the birth of Ganges. It is said that when the Ganges fell from heaven, in response to the prayers of Bhagirathi, for the lustration of the ashes of the sixty thousand sons of Sagara, Siva caught its waters in His matted locks, lest their force should overwhelm the world; and indeed they wandered in His hair for ages before they reached the earth at all. There may be more in this story than appears upon the surface; yet, regarded as a myth, it seems to represent some vision of the mighty river's source amongst the forest-covered slopes of the Himalayas, where is situated Siva's paradise, the heavenly Kailasa. Perhaps the most noticeable thing about this figure is its wonderful repose and graciousness. In the two ears are earrings of different patterns. This symbolism, characteristic both of *Mahayana* Buddhist and Hindu images, indicates the double nature, male and female, of the Divine Life. (47)

Siva Gangadhara, Elephanta Island

WORSHIP OF SIVA

The story of Sundara Murti Swami, one of the four great Tamil Saivite hymn writers (fl. about 700 A.D.) is briefly as follows: Born at Tirunavalur in the Madras presidency, he was adopted by the king, but brought up as a learned *brahman*. When he grew older, a suitable marriage was arranged. Arrayed in bridal attire, he rode out to the marriage. Then Siva, "though He has neither form nor city nor name, yet for the sake of saving human souls, took shape and name as an aged *brahman* and came from Kailas to bar the way." Holding up a piece of written palm leaf, He claimed the boy as a family slave. A quarrel ensued, and the boy tore up the bond in anger, calling the old man mad. But this was only a copy of the original. Finally it was agreed that the original should be submitted to a committee of *brahmans* for inspection. It was found to be in the boy's grandfather's writing, and to bind himself and his descendants as slaves to the old man forever. Witnesses present had to admit their signature. It was agreed that the marriage must be stopped, and the boy must follow the old man as a slave. But where did He live? "Follow Me," said He. The boy did so, and He led the way into a Saiva temple and there disappeared. Then, appearing to the boy in a vision as Siva, with Parvati and Nandi, He claimed him as His devotee of old. Sundara Murti Swami worshipped the Lord with tears of bliss, feeling himself "like a rootless tree." Siva said: "My favorite worship is the singing of hymns; sing Tamil hymns now." The boy said he knew not how. "As you just now called Me madman," said the Lord "so let that be My name, and sing." So he sang the first hymn, of which the first verse runs:

O Madman, Wearer of the crescent moon, Lord and gracious One,
How comes it that I ever think on Thee, my heart remembering Thee always?
Thou hast placed the Veenai river on the south!
O Father dwelling in the fair city of Vennai Nallur.
Since I am Thy slave, how may I deny it? (47)

Siva's Night (*Siva Ratri*) is a fast day falling on the fourteenth day of Maga (February). For twenty-four hours the Saivite should abstain from food, drink, and sleep. *Puja* (offerings of flowers, fruit, and water) is offered to Siva every three hours of the day and night. If the picture does not actually stand for "Siva Ratri," it is properly described, in any case, as Siva *puja*, adoration of Siva. The picture represents a princess with two or more attendants making offerings at a mountain shrine at night. The *linga*, Siva's symbol, is seen on the right at the mouth of a little cave within which a light is burning. On to the *linga* falls a splashing stream of water from the rock, to form a rivulet that finally passes across the front of the picture, where its bank is lined with flowers and nodding sedges. This stream is the Ganges, that falls from heaven on to Siva's head, and thence to earth. Perhaps there is a further meaning in the picture. Just as the *yogi* in some Indian pictures stands for Siva Himself, so here, the princess adoring Siva may be Uma. There is a conscious air about the mountain and the forest. Uma is daughter of the mountain, she is Parvati. The half-hidden moon, even though full, suggests the crescent moon on Siva's brow; perhaps this reveals to us more than any other detail the picture's mysterious charm—the whole landscape is the living garment of Siva Himself. The *linga* is only a symbol, but He is everywhere. (47)

At a shrine to Siva, Mughal miniature, c. 1735

GANESHA

Ganesha or Ganapati, son of Siva and Parvati, is the god of wisdom, arts, and sciences; he is always represented with an elephant's head, and seated. His relationship with Siva is shown by the crescent moon and skull in his headdress and the third eye on his forehead. His attributes are a rosary, an axe, a piece of elephant tusk, and a dish from which he takes food with his trunk. He is essentially the Remover of Difficulties, invoked at the beginning of undertakings. His image is often placed over the doors of houses. He is easy to be approached, and is spoken of with affectionate familiarity. He is a god of success in physical, intellectual, and spiritual life. The concrete symbolism has been interpreted as follows: his restless trunk is for the enquiring mind; the combination of head and hand (trunk) are for the power of thought in action; his great stomach is that of one who digests all; his vehicle, a rat, shows his power of penetrating everywhere. The rosary is a sign of his relation to Siva in his ascetic aspect; the axe is the attribute of one who cuts his way through jungles (of opposition). (47)

The god Ganesha, Halebid region, 11th century

DEVI

Durga is a form of Devi (Uma, Parvati, etc.). She is represented as the destroyer of evil, in the form of the demon Mahisha. In one classic, she has eight arms, and stands on a kneeling buffalo, from whose neck the demon Mahishasura emerges in dwarf form. One hand holds the buffalo by the tail, another the demon by the hair; one bears a shield and others are broken away. Durga has a crescent moon and skull in the headdress, as Sakti of Siva. She wears sarong and bodice with lotus ornament, and the usual jewelry. She is represented as a woman of amazonian proportions, in active movement. In the well developed torso and powerful build we find a feminine type differing widely from the more usual types of India, where the waist is constricted. (47)

Remembering how the gods are shaped by men in their own image, the various types of representation of Devi seem to throw much light on the earlier Indian conceptions of woman. Here she is the Amazon or Valkyrie; in the Prajnaparamita, she is the embodiment of wisdom; in the Uma, she is essentially "feminine," though even here she is represented as expounding or teaching (perhaps explaining to Siva the duties of women—*Mahabharata*); as Kali she is the "Destroyer of Time." (47)

A feature typical of Hindu theology is the conception of the Two-in-One—*Purusa* and *Prakriti*, Siva-Sakti, Lakshmi-Narayana, etc.

Associated with the Lord is his consort, "Energy" or "Power," known variously as Devi Sakti, Uma, Parvati, etc. These male and female principles are often represented iconographically side by side, or the Sakti may be conceived as part of the god's form. In the same way every Hindu deity has a feminine counterpart or active power; Visnu for example, being associated with Lakshmi, Krishna with Radha and so on. (39)

Pattini Devi, 10th century

HANUMAN

Finally, we have to refer to the fine image of Hanuman now in the Indian Museum at South Kensington, to which it was presented by the late William Morris. In age this may be associated with the bronzes from Polonnaruva (10th-13th century). I know no representation of the monkey-god more impressive than this, or more pathetic in its combination of human or divine intelligence and affection, with an animal nature. (47)

Hanuman, bronze statue at the Indian Museum at South Kensington (now the Victoria & Albert Museum), London

4. PEOPLE

Sri Ramakrishna

SRI RAMAKRISHNA

Nothing, perhaps, so strangely impresses or bewilders a Christian student of Saint Ramakrishna's life as the fact that this Hindu of Hindus, without in any way repudiating his Hinduism, but for the moment forgetting it, about 1866 completely surrendered himself to the Islamic way, repeated the name of *Allah*, wore the costume and ate the food of a Mussalman. This self-surrender to what we should call in India the waters of another current of the single river of truth resulted only in a direct experience of the beatific vision, not less authentic than before. Seven years later Ramakrishna in the same way proved experimentally the truth of Christianity. He was now for a time completely absorbed in the idea of Christ, and had not room for any other thought. You might have supposed him to be a convert. What really resulted was that he could now confirm on the basis of personal experience, "I have also practiced all religions, Hinduism, Islam, Christianity, and I have also followed the paths of the different Hindu sects.—The lake has many shores. At one the Hindu draws water with a pitcher, and calls it *jala*, at another the Mussalman in leather bottles, and calls it *pani*, at a third the Christian finds what he calls 'water.'" (34)

Sri Ramakrishna

SRI RAMANA MAHARISHI

I have the highest respect for Ramana Maharishi and I think he ranks with Sri Ramakrishna. I should think it a great privilege to take the dust of his feet. (50)

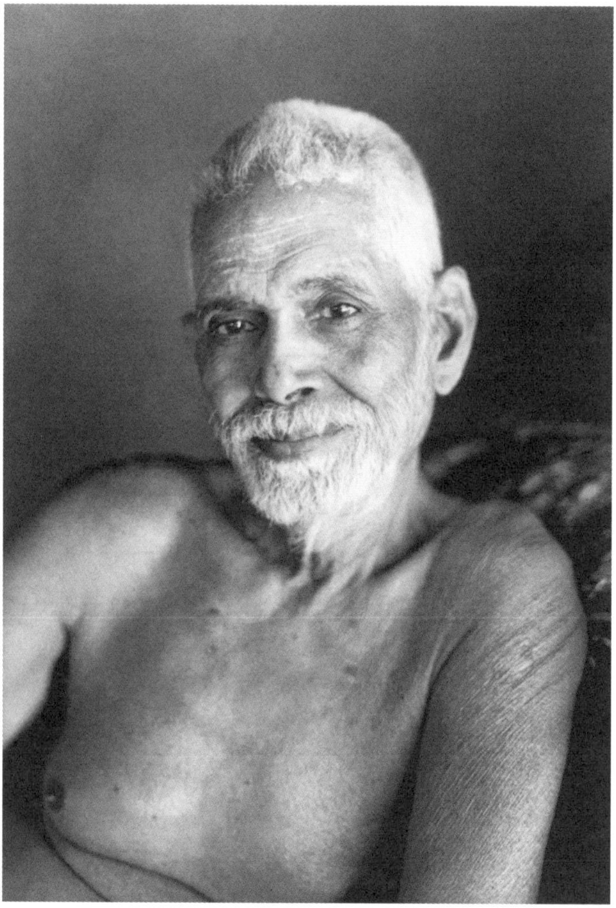

Sri Ramana Maharishi

SISTER NIVEDITA

Sister Nivedita, a most sincere disciple of Swami Vivekananda, who was himself a follower of the great Ramakrishna, brought to the study of Indian life and culture a sound knowledge of Western educational and social science, and an unsurpassed enthusiasm of devotion to the peoples and the ideals of the adopted country. Her chief works are *The Web of Indian Life*, almost the only fair account of Hindu society written in English, and *Kali the Mother*, where also for the first time the profound tenderness and terror of the Indian Mother-cult are presented to Western readers in such a manner as to reveal its true religious and social significance. Through these books Nivedita became more than merely an interpreter of India to Europe, but ever more, the inspiration of a new race of Indian students, no longer anxious to be Anglicized, but convinced that all real progress, as distinct from mere political controversy, must be based on national ideals, upon intentions already clearly expressed in religion and art. (29)

Sister Nivedita (right) with Sri Sarada Devi, wife of Sri Ramakrishna

MAHATMA GANDHI

I have the highest respect for Mahatma Gandhi's work in this field. By his advocacy of *satyagraha* he reminded India of her most ancient ideals and is not only a teacher for India but a *Jagat Guru*. But non-violence as he also knows, is not merely a matter of refraining from visibly violent actions; it is a matter of making peace with ourselves, one of learning to obey our inner man, for none but the outer man or ego is aggressive. (19)

Gandhi, despite all his errors, is the man of the age—our age. Gandhi is great because he has dared to speak of non-violence in a time of violence, of peace and brotherhood in a time of degradation and human destruction. He has spoken of man's highest inner quality, and though we, who are of limited vision, cannot expect to follow him we cannot refrain from admiring and even worshipping him—a man who is showing us a way which cannot be followed until mankind is tamed. (18)

It will not be overlooked that Mahatma Gandhi himself, so well known as a champion of the "untouchables," does not wish to do away with caste. (71)

Mahatma Gandhi, universally regarded as a great spiritual force in the world, would like to resolve the untouchables' problem, but still believes in the theory of the caste system. To do away with caste, to reduce all men to the condition of the modern proletarians who have no vocations but only "jobs" would not be a solution, but much rather a dissolution. (17)

To call a man Mahatma is to say that he has been liberated in this life (*jivan mukta*, corresponding to the Buddhist *drste dharme vimukta*) or in some life.... (12)

Our object in the present article has been to explain the word "Mahatma" historically. The name has been given to Gandhiji by common consent, perhaps in the general sense of the "saint." There can be no doubt that in some of its connotations, that of selflessness (with a higher sense than that of a mere unselflessness) for example, it can be properly applied to him. But we have not had in mind to discuss the applicability of the term in its full meaning to any individual: for that must ever remain secrecy between himself and God. (12)

Thought it worthwhile to call attention to a remarkable continuity of the Indian tradition in thinking of God as truth; a tendency from the *Rig Veda* to Gandhi. (56)

Mahatma Gandhi

JAWAHARLAL NEHRU

Nehru is the man of the moment because we have been caught unawares and unprepared, and he speaks a language the West understands. (18)

Zetland, in the *Legacy of India*, laments that after a hundred and fifty years of British rule in India "it comes as something of a shock to discover how little has been added during that time to the legacy of India in the (cultural) sense in which the word is here employed." Nehru, our Foreign Minister, has had to admit that, "I am a queer mixture of East and West, out of place everywhere, at home nowhere"; Jinnah knows little or nothing of Islam; theirs was an "Anglo-Indian" education. (38)

Jawaharlal Nehru with Mahatma Gandhi at a meeting of the Indian Congress, Bombay, 1946

RABINDRANATH TAGORE

It would be difficult to exaggerate the significance for Indian nationalism, of such heroic figures as that of Rabindranath Tagore, the Bengali poet, dramatist, and musical composer: "for nations are destroyed or flourish in proportion as their poetry, painting, and music are destroyed or flourish." The work of Rabindranath is essentially Indian in sentiment and form. It is at the same time modern. (4)

Vaisnava art is correspondingly humanistic, and it is from this school of thought that the poetry of Rabindranath Tagore derives. In it are echoed the teachings of such prophets as Sri Chaitanya, and poets such as Jayadev and Chandidas, who sung of the religion of love. (4)

Through all Rabindranath's songs there runs an undertone of sadness: this must always be so in the work of serious men. This sadness is not a gloom, but rather a secret joy, that perceives with unfaltering vision the splendid pageant of life, but looks upon death as an adventure awaiting no less glorious achievement. (4)

Ananda Coomaraswamy with Rabindranath Tagore

RAVI VARMA

It has indeed been Ravi Varma's reward for choosing Indian subjects, that he has been to some degree a true nationalizing influence; but had he been also a true artist with the gift of great imagination, this influence must have been tenfold deeper and greater. He is the landmark of a great opportunity, not perhaps wholly missed, but ill availed of; melodramatic conceptions, want of restraint, anecdotal aims and a lack of Indian feeling in the treatment of sacred and epic subjects are his faults. His art is not truly national—he merely plays with local color. His gods and heroes are men cast in a very common mold, who find themselves in situations for which they lack a proper dignity. The resulting degradation of what should be heroic and ideal types is quite unpardonable. Ravi Varma's pictures, in a word, are not national art; they are such as any European student could paint, after only a superficial study of Indian life and literature. A reaction from these ideals is represented by what has been called the New School of Indian Painting founded by Abanindranath Tagore. (5)

Rama's Wrath, painting by Ravi Varma

NANDALAL BOSE

Nandalal is the ideal *guru.* Perhaps the man in him is even greater than the artist. It is an education itself to know him as well as a great pleasure. In his everyday life, he is simple even as an ordinary villager. The coarsest *khaddar* clothes him. (59)

Mr. Nandalal Bose is already well known as one of the most brilliant of the still too small group of Indian painters who following Mr. Tagore's lead, have shown that the Indian creative interest is still a living power, and that there is a deeper meaning in Indian nationalism than a mere demand for rights. (60)

Left: *Radha's Longing*; *Right*: *Siva drinking World Poison*
paintings by Nandalal Bose

UDAY SHANKAR

Now what has Shankar done? Much of Shankar's training has been European, and he is much more individually the "artist" in a modern sense than is the Indian virtuoso whose art is one of fixed ends and ascertained means of operation, not to be arbitrarily modified in accordance with any personal taste. One of Shankar's assistants has been a European, though qualified by a remarkable adaptability. But if Shankar's performances are not just what could still be seen in India, neither would it be fair to say that his art is not authentically Indian dancing or acting. Shankar is after all an Indian, and a man of artistic integrity. His training in Europe represents only a part of his resources; he has studied obediently and patiently as the disciple (we use the word advisedly) of Indian professionals, and has assimilated rather than merely observed. In recent years he has studied with particular devotion the dramatic practice of Southern India, particularly in Malabar, where the art of the Kathakalis, of which an account was recently published in the *Illustrated London News*, has preserved better than anywhere else both the technique and the quality of the ancient drama. He uses an Indian technique to give expression to Indian themes, derived as in India from the inexhaustible material of the Epics, which are really Myths. He has brought with him groups of hereditary musicians, and enabled Americans to hear the instrumental music of India for the first time. Bearing in mind that Indian acting, dancing, and music are performed under conditions of patronage more like those under which European chamber music has developed than like those of the modern commercial stage, one may say that he has brought the Indian theater to America as sincerely and as really as was perhaps at all possible; and that he deserves all the credit for this, and all the appreciation, that he has received. (65)

Uday Shankar and Sinkie as Siva and Parvati

Uday Shankar

Coomaraswamy in India, c. 1909

AUTOBIOGRAPHICAL

Thirty years ago my father was the leading Tamil in Ceylon, and it will recur to most of you that he himself had become exceedingly Westernized. At that time it was necessary both that we should in some measure adapt ourselves to a changed environment and also prove ourselves capable of equaling the attainments of Western men on their own lines. Had he lived, I cannot doubt that (like my cousins, Messrs. Arunachalam and Ramanathan, who also at one time trod the same path) he would have seen that we were liable to overshoot the mark and he would have been the first to preserve and protect the national ideals and Eastern traditions, with which our lives and those of our forefathers are inextricably bound up. It is therefore fitting that his son should carry on such work. Of my mother I may say that it was her hope that her marriage with my father would contribute to a better understanding and sympathy between English and Tamils for whom she felt great admiration and affection and I may say I am now working for a cause which has her fullest sympathy. (43)

When I came to Ceylon for the third time, nearly four years ago, I was still to all intents and purposes an Englishman, but while I have lost nothing of my affection for English literature and art, I have been reborn as a child of India, and have in some measure returned to the ancestral home as a child to its parents. (43)

I was not bred on Indian soil, yet now when I go about my friends in India, I often find they quarrel with me because I am much too Indian in my ways of thinking for their anglicized tastes. (*)

As the only speaker here not "from within the Anglo-Saxon tradition" I have been asked to "participate as a critic of Western ideas and attitudes" and I mean to do just that. But I also claim to be a representative of both the cultures I inherit, and I hope it will not be thought that the critical function to which I am committed reflects any merely intransigent attitude on my part; and I think it may be fair to myself, and to others present, to say that I am in fact almost as much of a Platonist and Medievalist as I am an Orientalist, and that in writing on cultural relations my work has always been directed towards an exposition of the common metaphysical tradition that underlies both cultures, European and Asiatic, and to showing that their differences, however great, are accidental rather than essential, and

of comparatively modern origin, and so not necessarily insurmountable; although I would agree that to bring about a really mutual understanding much good will and even more good work, intellectual rather than moral, may be needed. (10)

When I survey the life of India during the last 3,000 years and bear in mind her literature, traditions, and ideals, the searchings of her philosophers, and the work of her artists, the music of her sons and daughters, and the nobility of the religion they have evolved, and when from these elements I form in my mind a picture of an ideal India and an ideal earthly life, I confess it is difficult for me to imagine a more powerful source of inspiration, a deeper well of truth to draw upon. (43)

By the way, if you must say something, do not try to whitewash me. I have lived in very confused times, I have played the game as thoroughly and completely as necessity demanded. I have tried to take the pleasure and the pain, what the world approves and disapproves with equilibrium. Where is the man who has not made mistakes? To have lived in any other way would have been to evade the issue—had this not been required of me it would not have happened. I am not a Victorian. By meeting the conflict one comes to know the better from the worse and learns to discriminate. These indeed are times of transition when the very contraries of which the walls of the universe are made cease to be good and evil—for we "modern" Europeans are always pitching two evils, one against the other. (74)

Every man holds dear his Homeland. As for me, my love for India is my destiny. I feel for her what a child feels towards her parents. (*)

Look at this house. I don't have a radio because I can't stand one. The longer I have lived in the United States the more Indian I have become and therefore I shall be happy when I settle down in India. (18)

If I were not getting solid food out of scholarship, I would drop it tomorrow, and spend my days fishing and gardening! (20)

As for myself I will only say that no day passes in which I do not read the Scriptures and the works of the great philosophers of all ages so far as they are accessible to me in modern languages and in Latin, Greek, and Sanskrit. I am wholly convinced that there is one truth that shines through

them all in many shapes, a truth greater in glory by far than can be circumscribed by any creed or confined by the walls of any church or temple. (11)

I have myself been completely dissolved and broken up by [Gregorian chant], and had the same experience when reading aloud Plato's *Phaedo*. That cannot have been an "aesthetic" emotion, such as could have been felt in the presence of some insignificant work of art, but represents the shock of conviction that only an intellectual art can deliver, the body-blow that is delivered by any perfect and therefore convincing statement of truth. (26)

My business is to do His business. Remember, "There is nothing in the three worlds, that should be done by Me, nor anything unattainable that might be attained; yet I mingle in action" (*Bhagavad Gita*, III, 22). (74)

My wife and I are returning to live in Northern India for the rest of our lives. This will be by the end of 1948. We mean to live in *retirement*. I shall not take part in any public functions or affairs whatever but individuals who wish to do so will be free to visit us. (19)

I have used the tools of the present age, that is my scientific training, which I took seriously, to be used without a bias. My life, my work, and my understanding follow a sequence and are predominantly logical. (50)

I am not a reformer or a propagandist. I don't think for myself.... I am not putting forward any new or private doctrines or interpretations.... I spend my time trying to understand some things that I regard as immutable truths; in the first place, for my own sake, and secondly for that of those who can make use of my results. For me, there are certain axioms, principles, or values beyond question; my interest is not in thinking up new ones, but in the application of those that are. (9)

I, too, have a vocation, which is much rather one of research in the field of the significance of the universal symbols of the *Philosophia Perennis* than one of apology for or polemic on behalf of doctrines that must be believed if they are to be understood, and must be understood if they are to be believed. (71)

To be President of the United States is not in my power, nor would it give me any pleasure; on the other hand, I am one of the few whose work is their delight, I am contented and having this experience, I say that any civilization stands self-condemned in which men have to earn their living in any other way than by doing what they would rather be doing than anything else in the world. (17)

I have never placed nationalism above religion. (19)

I am grateful to you for reading my books. Their contents are not "mine" so I have no hesitation as to their value in that respect, but on the other hand I am well aware of their deficiencies in exposition, at least in parts. (72)

KEY TO SOURCES

The numbers indicate the sources. An asterisk is given where the source is not given.

1. Ceylon National Review (1907)
2. History of Indian and Indonesian Art
3. The Dance of Siva
4. Art and *Swadeshi*
5. Essays in National Idealism
6. Arts and Crafts of India and Ceylon
7. Mediaeval Sinhalese Art
8. Blackfriars (1939)
9. Letter to Herman Goetz
10. The Heritage of the English-Speaking peoples and their Responsibility
11. Seventieth Birthday Speech
12. Mahatma Gandhi—60th Birthday Volume
13. Ceylon National Review (1908)
14. East and West (Speech at the Jaffna Hindu College, 1906)
15. The Asian Legacy and American Life
16. Art, Man, and Manufacture
17. The Religious Basis of the Forms of Indian Society
18. Interview with Dr. S. Chandrasekhar
19. Letter to S. Durai Raja Singam
20. Letter to H.G. Rawlinson
21. Christian and Oriental Philosophy of Art
22. Is Art a Superstition or a Way of Life?
23. The Aims of Indian Art
24. Figures of Speech or Figures of Thought?
25. Am I My Brother's Keeper?
26. *Samvega*: Aesthetic Shock
27. The Aims of Indian Art
28. Hinduism and Buddhism
29. Myths of the Hindus and Buddhists
30. The Transformation of Nature in Art
31. Buddha and the Gospel of Buddhism

32. Letter to Walter Shewring
33. The Common Wisdom of the World
34. The Paintings of Rabindranath Tagore
35. Indian Independence Day Speech
36. Asia and the Americas (1943)
37. Reactions to Art in India
38. The "Curse" of Foreign Rule
39. Mediaeval and Modern Hinduism
40. Paths that Lead to the Same Summit: Some Observations on Comparative Religion
41. The Bugbear of Democracy, Freedom, and Equality
42. The Gods of India
43. Two Addresses
44. A University Course in Indian Art
45. Understanding Indian Art
46. *Vidyapati*
47. The Oriental View of Women
48. Memoirs of the Colombo Museum—Bronzes from Ceylon
49. Aims of Indian Art
50. Coomaraswamy: The Man and His Message (1948)
51. Art in Indian Life
52. The Dance of Siva
53. The Shield (1911)
54. Art of Eastern Asia
55. The Deeper Meaning of the Struggle
56. Letter to John Clark Archer
57. The Bugbear of Literacy
58. Why Exhibit Works of Art?
59. India (1936)
60. The Modern Review (1909)
61. Note by A.K.C. in Family Collection
62. Letter to James Marshall Plumer
63. Letter to Stanley Nott
64. The Indian Review (1909)
65. The Magazine of Art (1937)
66. The Artist's Responsibility
67. Love and Art
68. *Yaksha*s
69. A New Approach to the Vedas

70. Letter to B.S. Sitholey
71. Letter to Jean David
72. Letter to Howard Hollis
73. Foreword to Prospectus of the College of Notre Dame Workshop
74. Some Recollections and References to Ananda Coomaraswamy—Doña Luisa Coomaraswamy
75. Hindustan Review (1914)
76. The Message of the East
77. The Artist's Responsibility.
78. Rajput Painting
79. On the Loathly Bride
80. Vedanta and Western Tradition
81. Gotama the Buddha
82. The Nature of Buddhist Art
83. The Pertinence of Philosophy
84. The Symbolism of the Dome
85. Symptom, Diagnosis, and Regimen
86. Understanding Hindu Art
87. The Nature of "Folklore" and "Popular Art"
88. Beauty and Truth
89. Who is "Satan" and Where is "Hell"?

GLOSSARY OF SOME INDIAN WORDS

Acarya: Teacher; master.

Ahimsa: Non-violence (*a*, privative; *himsa*, violence). This is an ancient Hindu precept, proclaimed by Buddha, by followers of Visnu, and by Mahavira, founder of Jainism.

Alpa-Buddhi Jana: An uninitiated reader.

Bhagavad Gita: The Song of the Divine Lord. This is a poem of 700 stanzas and part of the *Mahabharata*.

Brahman: The priestly caste; also, the absolute Real.

Bhakta: A devotee; a follower of the way of love or devotion (*bhakti*).

Dharma: Religion or religious duty.

Dharmasastra: The ancient Hindu law books; also referred to as the "Laws of Manu."

Gandhi: Gandhi, Mohandas Karamchand (1869-1948). Known as Mahatma ("great soul"). Leader of Indian Nationalist movement; frequently fasted during six and a half years in prison; exponent and exemplar of *satyagraha* and *ahimsa*; crusader for India's "untouchables" and traditional Hindu values.

Gandhiji: A title of respect for Gandhi, the *ji* corresponding to "sir" or "mister." Sometimes the word *Mahatmaji* was used.

Gath: A bathing area, usually with steps leading to a pond or river, used for religious purposes.

Gita: Song. See *Bhagavad Gita.*

Guna: An attribute or cosmic quality of *Prakriti*, of which all created things are woven. The three *gunas* are: *sattva* (purity, light), *rajas* (activity, expansiveness), and *tamas* (inertia, heaviness).

Guru: A spiritual guide.

Isvara: "Lord"; the personal God.

Jagat Guru: World teacher (*jadat*, world; *guru*, teacher, master, guide).

Jainism: An Indian religious system founded in the 6th century B.C. by Mahavira.

Kshatriya: The royal and warrior caste.

Lila: The creation of the world through the divine "play."

Linga(m): The male organ of generation as a symbol of the creative power of Siva.

Mahabharata: The national epic of which Krishna is the divine hero. The *Bhagavad Gita* is part of this epic.

Mahatma: Great soul (*maha*, great; *atma*, soul).

Maya: Illusion, appearance. The phenomenal world as an illusory veil covering over the abolute *Brahman*.

Mimamsa: A philosophical school of Hinduism emphasizing the importance of ritual action rather than contemplation.

Naga: Serpent.

Nandalal Bose: (1882-1966). A foremost painter.

Nataraja: Siva as the cosmic dancer.

Nehru: Nehru, Jawaharlal (1889-1964). Prime Minister of India 1947-1964. With Gandhi, leader of the Nationalist movement, spent nine years in jail for political "crimes"; erudite interpreter of Indian and world history; developed Indian central government and neutralist foreign policy.

Nivedita: (1867-1911). A disciple of Sri Ramakrishna and Swami Vivekananda.

Pandita: A scholar learned in the scriptures.

Prakriti: The fundamental, "feminine" substance or material cause of all things.

Purusa: The informing or shaping principle of creation; the "masculine" demiurge or fashioner of the universe.

Raja Ravi Varna: (1848-1906). A painter whose main topics were Indian subjects, but whose pictures were not considered national art by some art critics.

Ramayana: An ancient Hindu epic relating the story of Rama and his wife Sita.

Rasa: Taste; feeling or emotion as the spiritual perception or experience of art.

Rishi: Seer.

Sakti: The consort of Siva; creative "power" expressed in the form of divine femininity.

Sannyasin(i): A renunciate; one who has renounced all formal ties to social life.

Satyagraha: The philosophy and practice of non-violent resistance (*satya*, truth; *graha*, force) developed by Mahatma Gandhi.

Shaivite: Devotee of Siva; see also Nataraja.

Sri Ramakrishna: (1836-1886). Hindu mystic; devotee of the goddess Kali; experienced the spirit of Islam and Christianity, and emphasized the unity of religions; considered by many to be an *avatar*.

Sri Ramana Maharshi: (1879-1950). Twentieth-century south Indian mystic; achieved spiritual realization at seventeen years of age; settled at Tiruvannamalai, where an *ashram* grew up around him for more than fifty years; explained spiritual realization in terms of Advaita Vedanta.

Stupa: A Buddhist burial mound, usually containing relics of the Buddha or a revered saint.

Sudra: The laborer caste.

Swadeshi: Belonging to, or made in, one's own country (*swa*, self; *deshi*, country).

Swaraj: Self-government; independence (*swa*, self; *raj*, government).

Tagore: Tagore, Ravindranath (1861-1941). Poet of modern India.

Tevaram: A Tamil Saivite devotional hymn.

Uday Shankar: (1900-1977). World famous Indian dancer.

Vaishya: The merchant, peasant, and craftsman caste.

Vaisnava: A devotee of Visnu.

Vedas: Earliest Hindu religious hymns.

Yoga: As formulated by Patanjali and based on the Sankya system, a physical, mental, and spiritual discipline leading to *samadhi* or union; more generally, any one of several disciplines such as *karma-yoga* (the path of action), *jnana-yoga* (the path of knowledge), *bhakti-yoga* (the path of devotion), and *dhyana-yoga* (the path of meditation).

Yogi: A practitioner of *yoga*; one who has realized the goal of *yoga*.

For a glossary of all key foreign words used in books published by World Wisdom, including metaphysical terms in English, consult: www.DictionaryofSpiritualTerms.org.
This on-line Dictionary of Spiritual Terms provides extensive definitions, examples, and related terms in other languages.

BIOGRAPHICAL NOTES

ANANDA K. COOMARASWAMY was born in 1877, the son of Sir Mutu Coomaraswamy, one of the leading men of Sri Lanka, and Lady Elizabeth Clay Bibi, an Englishwoman from an aristocratic Kent family. After graduating from London University with Honors in Geology, he became—at age 25—Director of the Mineralogical Survey in Ceylon (Sri Lanka). His interests were soon, however, to be consumed by the arts and crafts of the region, which he expertly interpreted in the light of their underlying metaphysical principles. In 1917 Dr. Coomaraswamy relocated to the USA where he became Keeper of Indian and Islamic Art at the Boston Museum of Fine Arts, establishing a large collection of Oriental artifacts and presenting lectures on their symbolic and metaphysical meaning. An encounter with the seminal writings of Traditionalist author René Guénon served to confirm and strengthen his view of the perspective of the perennial philosophy, or "transcendent unity of religions"—the view that all authentic Heaven-sent religions are paths that lead to the same summit. From this period onwards Dr. Coomaraswamy began to compose his mature—and undoubtedly most profound—works, adeptly expounding the perspective of the perennial philosophy by drawing on his unparalleled knowledge of the arts, crafts, mythologies, cultures, folklores, symbolisms, and religions of the Orient and the Occident. In 1947 he had planned to retire from his position as curator at the Boston Museum of Fine Arts and return to India, with the intention of completing a new translation of the *Upanisad*s and taking on *sannyasa* (renunciation of the world). These plans, however, were cut short by his sudden and untimely death.

WHITALL N. PERRY was born in 1920 of a prominent Boston Quaker family. Travels in his youth through Europe, the Near, Middle, and Far East sparked an interest in Platonism and Vedanta, which brought him under the personal influence of Ananda K. Coomaraswamy. He spent five years in Egypt in close contact with René Guénon, after whose death he moved to Switzerland with his family, where he became a close associate of Frithjof Schuon for many years. In addition to his monumental *A Treasury of Traditional Wisdom*, he contributed articles on metaphysics, cosmology, and modern counterfeits of spirituality to various journals, several of which were collected together to form his book *Challenges to a Secular Society*. He has been referred to as "the most authoritative traditionalist of American background," and "a latter-day transcendentalist in the tradition of Emerson and Thoreau." Whitall Perry died in 2005.

S. DURAI RAJA SINGAM (1904-c. 1995) was a Malaysian scholar and friend of Ananda K. Coomaraswamy. He was the editor of numerous Indian works on or by Coomaraswamy, including *Homage to Ananda K. Coomaraswamy: A Garland of Tributes* (1948), *Homage to Ananda K. Coomaraswamy: A Memorial Volume* (1952), *Ananda Coomaraswamy: Remembering and Remembering Again and Again* (1974), and *Ananda Kentish Coomaraswamy: A Bibliographical Record* (1981), as well as *The Life and Writings of Sir Mutu Coomaraswamy* (1973).

JOSEPH A. FITZGERALD studied Comparative Religion at Indiana University, where he also earned a Doctor of Jurisprudence degree. He is a professional editor whose previous publications include *Of the Land and the Spirit: The Essential Lord Northbourne on Ecology and Religion* (with Christopher James), *Honen the Buddhist Saint: Essential Writings and Official Biography*, *The Essential Sri Anandamayi Ma: Life and Teachings of a 20th Century Saint from India*, *The Cheyenne Indians: Their History and Lifeways*, *A Christian Woman's Secret: A Modern-Day Journey to God*, and *An Illustrated Introduction to Taoism: The Wisdom of the Sages*. He lives with his wife and daughters in Bloomington, Indiana.

INDEX

Other Titles in the Perennial Philosophy Series by World Wisdom

The Betrayal of Tradition: Essays on the Spiritual Crisis of Modernity, edited by Harry Oldmeadow, 2005

Borderlands of the Spirit: Reflections on a Sacred Science of Mind, by John Herlihy, 2005

A Buddhist Spectrum: Contributions to Buddhist-Christian Dialogue, by Marco Pallis, 2003

A Christian Pilgrim in India: The Spiritual Journey of Swami Abhishiktananda (Henri Le Saux), by Harry Oldmeadow, 2008

The Essential Ananda K. Coomaraswamy, edited by Rama P. Coomaraswamy, 2004

The Essential Martin Lings, edited by Reza Shah-Kazemi and Emma Clark, 2012

The Essential René Guénon, edited by John Herlihy, 2009

The Essential Seyyed Hossein Nasr, edited by William C. Chittick, 2007

The Essential Sophia, edited by Seyyed Hossein Nasr and Katherine O'Brien, 2006

The Essential Titus Burckhardt: Reflections on Sacred Art, Faiths, and Civilizations, edited by William Stoddart, 2003

Every Branch in Me: Essays on the Meaning of Man, edited by Barry McDonald, 2002

Every Man An Artist: Readings in the Traditional Philosophy of Art, edited by Brian Keeble, 2005

Figures of Speech or Figures of Thought? The Traditional View of Art, by Ananda K. Coomaraswamy, 2007

A Guide to Hindu Spirituality, by Arvind Sharma, 2006

Introduction to Sufism: The Inner Path of Islam, by Éric Geoffroy, 2010

Introduction to Traditional Islam, Illustrated: Foundations, Art, and Spirituality, by Jean-Louis Michon, 2008

Islam, Fundamentalism, and the Betrayal of Tradition: Essays by Western Muslim Scholars, edited by Joseph E.B. Lumbard, 2004, 2009

Journeys East: 20th Century Western Encounters with Eastern Religious Traditions, by Harry Oldmeadow, 2004

Light From the East: Eastern Wisdom for the Modern West, edited by Harry Oldmeadow, 2007

Living in Amida's Universal Vow: Essays in Shin Buddhism, edited by Alfred Bloom, 2004

Maintaining the Sacred Center: The Bosnian City of Stolac, by Rusmir Mahmutćehajić, 2011

Of the Land and the Spirit: The Essential Lord Northbourne on Ecology and Religion, edited by Christopher James and Joseph A. Fitzgerald, 2008

On the Origin of Beauty: Ecophilosophy in the Light of Traditional Wisdom, by John Griffin, 2011

Paths to the Heart: Sufism and the Christian East, edited by James S. Cutsinger, 2002

Remembering in a World of Forgetting: Thoughts on Tradition and Postmodernism, by William Stoddart, 2008

Returning to the Essential: Selected Writings of Jean Biès, translated by Deborah Weiss-Dutilh, 2004

Science and the Myth of Progress, edited by Mehrdad M. Zarandi, 2003

Seeing God Everywhere: Essays on Nature and the Sacred, edited by Barry McDonald, 2003

Singing the Way: Insights in Poetry and Spiritual Transformation, by Patrick Laude, 2005

The Spiritual Legacy of the North American Indian: Commemorative Edition, by Joseph E. Brown, 2007

Sufism: Love & Wisdom,
edited by Jean-Louis Michon and Roger Gaetani, 2006

The Timeless Relevance of Traditional Wisdom,
by M. Ali Lakhani, 2010

The Underlying Religion: An Introduction to the Perennial Philosophy,
edited by Martin Lings and Clinton Minnaar, 2007

Unveiling the Garden of Love: Mystical Symbolism in Layla Majnun and Gita Govinda, by Lalita Sinha, 2008

Wisdom's Journey: Living the Spirit of Islam in the Modern World,
by John Herlihy, 2009

Ye Shall Know the Truth: Christianity and the Perennial Philosophy,
edited by Mateus Soares de Azevedo, 2005

Other Titles on Hinduism by World Wisdom

A Christian Pilgrim in India: The Spiritual Journey of Swami Abhishiktananda (Henri Le Saux), by Harry Oldmeadow, 2008

The Essential Sri Anandamayi Ma: Life and Teachings of a 20th CenturyIndian Saint, by Alexander Lipski and Sri Anandamayi Ma, 2007

The Essential Swami Ramdas: Commemorative Edition, compiled by Susunaga Weeraperuma, 2005

The Essential Vedanta: A New Source Book of Advaita Vedanta, edited by Eliot Deutsch and Rohit Dalvi, 2004

A Guide to Hindu Spirituality, by Arvind Sharma, 2006

Introduction to Hindu Dharma, by the 68th Jagadguru of Kanchi, edited by Michael Oren Fitzgerald, 2008

Lamp of Non-Dual Knowledge & Cream of Liberation: Two Jewels of Indian Wisdom, translated by Swami Sri Ramanananda Saraswathi, 2003

The Original Gospel of Ramakrishna, by Mahendra Nath Gupta, 2011

Paths to Transcendence: According to Shankara, Ibn Arabi & Meister Eckhart, by Reza Shah-Kazemi, 2006

The Power of the Sacred Name: Indian Spirituality Inspired by Mantras, by V. Raghavan, edited by William J. Jackson, 2011

Timeless in Time: Sri Ramana Maharshi, by A.R. Natarajan, 2006

Tripura Rahasya: The Secret of the Supreme Goddess, translated by Swami Sri Ramanananda Saraswathi, 2002

Unveiling the Garden of Love: Mystical Symbolism in Layla Majnun & Gitagovinda, by Lalita Sinha, 2009